FACE LANGUAGE

ROBERT L. WHITESIDE

FACE

LANGUAGE

ILLUSTRATIONS BY CLAUDIA ROMPEL

A World of Books That Fill a Need

FREDERICK FELL PUBLISHERS, INC.   NEW YORK

Library of Congress Cataloging in Publication Data

Whiteside, Robert L
 Face language.

 1. Physiognomy. 2. Facial expression. I. Title.
BF851.W55 1974   138   74 4418
ISBN 0-8119-0231-5

For information address:
Frederick Fell Publishers, Inc.
386 Park Avenue South
New York, N. Y. 10016
Library of Congress Catalog Card No. 74-4418
Published simultaneously in Canada by
George J. McLeod, Limited, Toronto 2B, Ontario
MANUFACTURED IN THE UNITED STATES OF AMERICA
International Standard Book Number 0-8119-0231-5

CONTENTS

FOREWORD

This book was designed as a working manual to help you when you encounter other people face-to-face. It will sharpen your perceptions in many ways: You will learn what pleases some people and offends others; you will be able to anticipate others' reactions to specific situations and influence their decisions.

Learning the techniques of FACE LANGUAGE will be extremely valuable to you in your home life, your business or professional life, your social life, and your sex life—because in them you will find realistic, practical tools applicable to all the day-to-day situations that are important to you.

You will also gain from this book a deeper understanding and appreciation of *yourself,* as the unique individual *you* are. Like your fingerprints, *you* are different from everyone else on earth. You will pay more attention to your own special attributes. And, you will better understand *your* personality and *your* temperament—with an immediate, dynamic and down-to-earth method that you can put into action *now.*

—ROBERT L. WHITESIDE

INTRODUCTION

Everybody is engaged in selling. You may be selling real estate. You may be trying to persuade your boss to try out an idea. Or you may be trying to convince your girl friend that you really care for her. As a pedestrian, you may just be catching the eye of an approaching motorist and getting the nod from him that he will wait for you while you hurry safely in front of him to catch your waiting bus. Every day, you try to sell someone on something that means a lot to you, and understanding the principles of face language will enable you to succeed more in the selling of yourself and your ideas and desires, each day. An understanding of these concepts is invaluable, because everyone is built differently and responds to situations differently.

You will learn from this book many ways to read other people's face language which you can put into action at once. You will gain many new insights, enhanced by graphic illustrations.

Let us look at some of these concepts in a preliminary way. For example, if the person with whom you're dealing has worry lines, these vertical lines mean that you had better be careful in your dealings with him if you want to succeed. You must be ON TIME (not early, not late). You must be exact in your statements. Don't say, "It's about seven hundred dollars," but say, "This model runs $697.83." Be neatly dressed. Have ready for him every small detail you can anticipate he might think of or require. Be smooth, well-prepared, and free-wheeling. Make no

Without knowing face language, you recognize the beauty of this lovely young woman, and sense her charm. But with the knowledge you will gain in this book, you would know also, even before you spoke to her that she is warm-hearted, conscientious, is well equipped with self-confidence, expresses herself well . . . and that her tastes are for quality rather than for quantity.

problems, such as worrying where to put your raincoat . . . he's a worrier and will create enough problems by himself. In short, be at your best.

If your boss has worry lines up and down between his eyebrows, and says he wants the reports in by the *second* day of the month, he doesn't mean the morning of the *third* day. Pleasing him in little things like that will win more promotions for you than bringing in a large new sales account. Face it— you are dealing with a fuss-budget, so make the most of it. If he has mentioned that there should be a one inch margin around your typed material, provide that one inch margin, impeccably . . . it will pay off, come end-of-year bonus time, because when YOU come to his mind, he will think of you as someone who is REALLY COOPERATIVE, and who gets his ideas. (In dealing with him, it's like the humorist said, "When in Rome, be a Roman candle.")

Another factor of face language available for your benefit is an indication of the individual's tendency toward brevity or verbosity by the size of his lips. If he has thin, tight lips, he is *concise*—and he wants you to be concise, too.

Such a man, with a mouth like a bear trap, doesn't waste words . . . and he doesn't want you to. (He doesn't waste time, either.) With him, make it short-and-sweet. This doesn't mean being grim . . . it's always better to smile. But it does mean to pick a few well-chosen words in which to get your proposal across.

A saleswoman was asked at a Salt Lake City breakfast meeting of her merchandising group, "How are you always Number One in sales?" Her reply was that she understood individuals' different natures from their faces. "If the person who comes to the door has small lips, get your point across quickly . . . if she has large, full lips, you have much more time —and she may even invite you in for cider and doughnuts before it's over!"

Think of the people you know. Those with large, loose lips indeed do take more time to cover the subject. And they are freer in handing out what they have to hand out. They are more likely, voluntarily, to stay late or work Saturdays.

One California student of face language went to the Long Beach pike on a holiday. Hungry for a hamburger, he looked through the hamburger stands and found a large-lipped fry-chef, with whom he placed his order . . . and received one of the most generous-sized hamburgers he'd ever enjoyed!

You will soon notice that the full-lipped individuals with whom you deal are more outgoing and sympathetic . . . and that the thin-lipped people are more brief and efficient. If you understand face language, your feelings won't be hurt when you're visiting New York City and you ask a tight-mouthed native, "Which way is Lexington Avenue?" and he merely points, without saying a word. You know that for him, that's verbose enough. Obviously, panhandlers waste their time if they try to put the touch on tight-lipped people.

Tight-lipped people can direct their generosity. The thin-lipped man may give his son a convertible with which to go to college. But nobody else had better try to get him to provide *him* with an automobile!

Let's turn from lips to eyes. If you try to sell someone who has large eyes, you're dealing with someone who is emotional. Your tone of voice is important. And your eyes must be friendly.

12

The large-eyed person takes everything you do (and the WAY you do it) as meaning whether you like him or her. Keep your voice down. Talk genuinely, and in a friendly manner. Use your smile. Mention people you both know. Talk about old times. Break bread.

If you work for someone you seldom see, but who you know has large eyes, do not write to him when you have a request you fear he may turn down. Go in person. Have lunch together. Talk about his family and yours. Laugh about funny things that happened when you were on a convention trip together. Then, in passing, mention, "Oh, by the way, if it's all right with you I'd like to try out this new idea that might help our production volume," and he's much less likely to refuse.

With face language, you can make points fast in your private life. If your wife has big "goo goo" eyes, she's full of feeling. She can be a lot of fun, but she's an incurable sentimentalist. To her, it's the whole world to have you smile at her when you come home, instead of frowning. Call her during the day, just to ask how she is. For her, always have a SPECIAL tone of voice, an intimate, loving, endearing voice that you reserve just for her. Bring her little gifts (with her initials on them, so she knows you have thought of her!). Leave sweet little notes for her where she's sure to find them—her heart sings then, and you bring out the best in her. Then, when your work requires that the family move to a new state, one she doesn't think she'll like, she'll romantically and loyally say, "Who cares? We have EACH OTHER, wherever we go!"

The color of the eyes doesn't matter. People with large, saucer eyes of gray or blue are just as emotional as those of dark brown.

The large-irised individual takes everything you do as meaning whether you like him or her, so it's a good idea not to turn down food. Even if you have just been to a smorgasbord, if you encounter an affectionate friend and he invites you to join him and his group at the banquet table, gladly accept. Join in the spirit. Eat what you can from your plate, or you will break his heart.

If your wife is large-eyed and you forget to kiss her good-bye, you have hurt her, because she is a romantic and needs a daily demonstration of how much you care.

Conversely, if the person with whom you're dealing has little, beady eyes, he is going to act more cold-blooded and businesslike. And he's going to expect you to be matter-of-fact and businesslike, too. He will give you a funny look if you start out the business conference by asking in a confidential tone, "How is little Kathy? . . . Did she get over that cold all right?" Look pleasant but stick to business. Have a better price than your competitor—this is what makes sense to him. (Whereas the large-eyed acquaintance is liable to buy from you regardless of price, if he has come to regard you as his real friend.)

You can see that if Mr. Small-Eyes also has thin lips and has heavy worry lines, then you had better be at your best when you try to persuade him about anything (for he is both business-like and exacting.) You know what you are up against, and can behave accordingly and be effective. And you are not hurt or offended at his brevity and fussiness, for you know that he is built in such a way that he is not going to act as warm and friendly to you as the large-eyed, full-lipped person with an unworried brow. Knowledge is power. Also, to understand is to forgive.

If your work has involved dealing face-to-face with many people, one at a time, you have been observant of them as individuals even before you found this book . . . and you are probably glad to discover, translated for you into everyday terms, usable findings from the research of the Interstate College of Personology. Salesmen, particularly, are quick to apply practical knowledge about people as individuals, for doing this results in more commissions.

I had the pleasure a while back of lecturing on face language for the Hinsdale, Illinois sales staff of a major insurance company (and also instructing each salesman personally on his own individual native pattern and how to best use his strong points to reach his potential.) Subsequently I did the same for the Pasadena, California agency of the same firm. The Hinsdale agency won the company's summer sales contest, and the Pasadena agency placed the most top men in the winter sales competition.

Try out the ideas which follow in this book, and gain the immediate benefits—whether your desired effective communication is formally selling, or whether it is persuasion of others in different matters. Not only will you be more effective. You will also enjoy much more dealing with them.

FACE LANGUAGE

1. NONVERBAL COMMUNICATION

"Your lips say 'No, no,'
But it's 'Yes, yes,' in your eyes—
I've been missing your kissing,
Just because I wasn't wise . . ."

So goes the song.

Your eyes tell so much about you, largely because they are so closely tied in with your emotions. You can feel without words. You can feel without thinking.

People are human beings. They have emotions. That is what makes them human, instead of just being machines or computers. And they do a lot more feeling than they do thinking. Often the "thinking" is used just to justify the emotions, as in the case of which candidate you are going to vote for.

It will reward you much more (in personal situations) to consider how the other person FEELS, than it will to give the same amount of attention to how he is THINKING.

Everybody needs two things. They need to be loved. And they need to feel worthwhile. Whether or not somebody likes you is important to you. And by what means are you to gauge whether someone likes you? Not by lengthy debates. The tone of voice . . . the look in the eye . . . the actions, tell more than words. "What you do speaks so loudly I can't hear what you say," someone said.

A frown and a sneer. A smile and a wink. There is no neutral in the world of feeling. And of course, the feelings are particularly important to the large-eyed, emotional individual. But they are important to all of us. In the small-eyed person they are just buried deeper. Sooner or later, they must come out.

You are interested in making more headway in life, and dealing better with other people. That is why you are reading this book. You have already become more observant of others, and as you put your knowledge to use, things will go your way more often. You are more alert to catch a hurt or puzzled look. Also, you more quickly catch the fleeting twinkle or smile. Keep up the good work! It will pay off handsomely.

Have you ever traveled abroad, in a country where you did not understand the language? If you have, then you know that you can get a great deal across just by smiling and pointing. And in your personal life, sometimes playing some music or bringing a flower will patch up a rift more easily than a discussion. How you FEEL about it, and getting that feeling across, is what counts.

If you have the aristocratic nose and businesslike mien, LOOK HAPPY when you bring your spouse breakfast in bed! If the recipient says, "I'm sorry to be putting you out—I don't want to be a bother to you," then you didn't get your INNER FEELINGS across. Better to ham it up a bit, and act like a stylish waiter or waitress . . . and get a smile out of your beloved, and a cherished moment to remember. If you spoil it

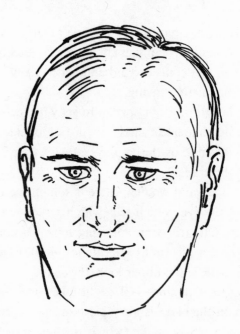

CRITICALNESS LOW
(but HARD)

all by dragging your feet and seeming to be just doing your duty, the other person is entitled to take you at your sign-language and exclaim, "Well, if you don't want to do it, don't do it!" (The gift without the giver is dead.) And this includes lovemaking.

You may have very well been missing the boat with your loved ones in this regard. But, no problem! The world of feelings is immediate in its action and response. I find that couples get back together much quicker than expected when they understand nonverbal communication and learn to play their cards better, provided they haven't meanwhile taken up with someone else. Someone to whom you are close can quickly forget an awful lot if you just come around and act friendly. This is the first step toward acting loving.

Even in business, it's important to get your feelings across. Once, while helping select clerks for a fashionable men's apparel store, I was told by the employer: "All I want is men who won't insult the trade!"

Between men and women, there is something that passes in the look of the eyes which tells whether they are interested in each other. Often it is an admiring look. Of course, since "love is boy chases girl (until she catches him!)" it is up to the woman to give the come-hither look, the sign or cue of interest or acceptance or willingness. Often "it takes one to spot one," and the man on the make is more alert and perceptive in spotting the woman on the make (which is often revealed by her uncertain eyes.) Or he may pursue the opening given by a look of loneliness . . . or the occasional brazen look of daring on the part of some hardened or sophisticated member of the feminine sex. Often a questioning look—a smile and the waiting for an answer, or the offering of refreshments—gets a message across better (and more safely than words.) And little argument can ever result.

The Europeans have much they could teach us about bowing, kissing hands, and curtseying. These gestures go a step beyond glances and smiles.

If you are thin-faced and self-conscious, you may have to expand your self-confidence a bit to put yourself forward and do such things. But you will surprise no one more than yourself. And if you do it in the right situations, you will receive ap-

When the colored part of the eye is large, and there is little white showing, here is the warm-hearted, affectionate individual, all of whose feelings are intense and close to the surface.

HIGH EMOTIONALITY (Affectionateness)

preciation and gratitude. People appreciate spirit. And nothing worthwhile was ever accomplished without enthusiasm. Watch the entertainers, singers, actresses and actors, and T.V. luminaries. You can learn a lot from them.

If you have little beady eyes and are not by nature much good at getting your feelings across, practice acting as if the other person did not understand English—and you HAD to get your feelings into your eyes and your thoughts into the expression of your face! Do not worry about it coming out exaggerated. By disposition you lean so much toward the other

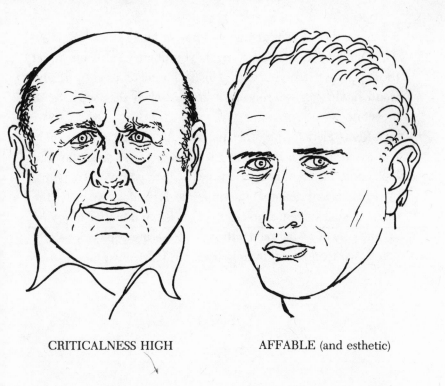

CRITICALNESS HIGH   AFFABLE (and esthetic)

direction, that it will only come out in a friendly fashion. The other person will just think you had a good night's sleep, or had just heard some good news. Life is largely a matter of getting the spirit across through the flesh.

In many situations in which you are dealing with a large-eyed, emotional person, few words are necessary. In fact, many times a five-word vocabulary will get your point across beautifully, if said sincerely: "Oh, too bad!" (if it's something to commiserate over), or, "Gee, great!" (if it's something over which to celebrate). This may sound too good to be true, but if you use these words genuinely, they will take you a long way.

One way to shut off contacts you don't want is not to let those people catch your eye. This technique is used by Hollywood luminaries wearing dark glasses when they want to be incognito.

Being alert to the other individual's expressions can help you avoid arguments. When the other person's face starts to look angry or red, it is a good time to lower your voice a couple of registers and genuinely ask for the HIS idea. At once, the threatened argument is averted. (This is not a matter of giving in, but only of giving recognition . . . lowering your voice shifts you down from the thinking area into the feeling area.)

2. EYES AND AREAS AROUND THE EYES

The eyes are the windows of your soul . . . and the mirror of your heart . . . and the gauges showing fleeting feelings and changes.

Think of the people you know who have the warmest and most sentimental nature, freely showing their feelings. They have large, brimming eyes (like the drawing on page 24). There is little white showing in *their* eyes. The iris or colored part is large. Those big "saucer" eyes tell you that the person is affectionate. All the feelings are on the surface. All the feelings are keen. This person will laugh more easily, cry more easily, show anger more vividly, show devastation of despair more completely, anguish more demonstratively, ecstasy more delightedly.

Try this out: If the person opposite you has noticeably large irises, smile and act in a friendly way, for that person will regard your expression and tone of voice as indicators of your feelings. (Such an individual thinks with the heart, not with the head.) If the emotional person says, "Can't you stay a bit and have a cup of coffee," however busy you are you had better take a sip, or the affectionate one will think you unfriendly. If you "break bread" with the affectionate individual, from then on you are considered a friend.

If your employer has large eyes, his family means a lot to him. Ask him whether Ronnie made the team. On the other hand, if your employer is built like the small-eyed man shown on page 32, don't ask him whether little Susie got over her cold all right, or he will give you a funny look. His feelings are deeply buried (better stick to business with him.) His children mean as much to him as anyone, but he has trouble getting sentiment into conversation.

Around the small-eyed person, man or woman, child or adult, expect little demonstrativeness. Rather, expect an awkwardness about the show of emotion. Give this person some encouragement to help get the heart more out on top. Some husbands are more big-hearted and emotional than their wives, and find that their wives are better at collecting past-due accounts in the business, or refusing credit to friends.

Another quality that shows in the eyes of the person facing you is magnetism (or the lack of it.)

The child or adult who has magnetism has sparkling eyes, like the illustration on page 41. There is a light in the eyes . . . "jewels in the eyes." Whether sweet or roguish, here is an alert individual who can get an audience wherever he or she goes . . . who stands out in a group . . . who attracts others . . . who is remembered . . . who gets a break. There is a spirit shining out—as if the person knew a happy secret.

The person with magnetism is more alert, more of a livewire, and everything else equal, more fun. They will enter with

ESTHETIC AND AFFABLE

more spirit into fun and joking . . . and be more exciting to be around, than individuals with lustreless, "dead-fish" eyes.

If you are in personnel work and selecting someone to be a receptionist or to do public relations work, choose the person with the sparkling eyes. Everyone perks up when they come around. Everyone is inclined to give them a break.

You may have a small son in school who has so much magnetism that he gets by on his charm—he gets by when he does things that other boys get sent to the principal for!

If your young-lady daughter has diamonds in her eyes,

The person whose upper eyelid you can plainly see, is a direct-actionist, once the way ahead is clear . . . and does not want to be bothered with the whys and wherefores.

30

What makes photographs and paintings so interesting? Why do you keep studying some of them? Often it is because the same person has contrasting sides to his nature. Here is a young woman with charm but who is an all-or-nothing person in whatever she does . . . she loves her home but is self-reliant and adventurous . . . she is sensitive physically but has abundant energy and a restless nature.

men realize how much fun she could be, and want to flirt with her. Tell her not to let anyone catch her eye with whom she does not want to be bothered, or she will have trouble getting rid of him.

On the more somber side of feelings, the eyes can also show unhappiness and gloom. Look at a melancholy countenance, where the white shows between the colored part of the eyes and the lower eyelid. Any person you meet who shows this unhappy extra white between the iris and the lower eyelid

LOW EMOTIONALITY

has unsolved problems weighing upon him. You may recall a whole book that was written on this trait alone, from Japanese research, entitled *San-Paku*. It pointed out that unless the person with the melancholy eyes resolved his problem constructively, he was heading for an even more unhappy situation.

Since the melancholy eyes are telling you that the person has problems weighing on him, do not expect him to be light-hearted and cheerful. If you comment, "What a beautiful day!," he is liable to answer, "What's good about it?"

If you get the melancholy person to one side and hear him out as someone really interested in him, he will open up. If your youngster has unhappy eyes, things seem too big for him, or he is doing something he is ashamed of. Draw him out at the proper moment, so he can unload. It does him good to know someone cares and that someone will back him up.

When you are hiring people, go easy on hiring those with gloomy eyes with extra white showing. Hire someone else instead without complications, who can put his best mind to his work.

Shifty eyes are another warning sign. The person who will not meet your eyes is less liable to be depended upon safely. He may not meet your gaze because he deliberately intends not to carry through. Or his shifty eyes may mean he is uncomfortable about the transaction because he is too self-conscious a person, or really isn't interested, or doesn't yet understand any real reason why he should do it (and yet hates to speak up and offend you). In any case, it amounts to a kind of deceitfulness. Don't hold your breath until he does what he gives the impression he will do or has promised. What you want from the other person is a clear, open, unworried gaze—neither shifty eyes nor a hard brazen stare.

Also remember that the person with glassy, bloodshot eyes is under a lot of pressure, and unpredictable in his actions.

Another trait more easily understood with face language is criticalness.

This breaks up more friendships than perhaps any other trait. We can all set our minds to it and deliberately think up strong and weak points in any situation. But the naturally

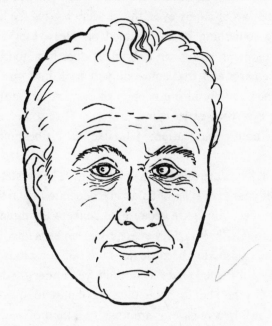

DISCRIMINATIVE (also, low analytical)

critical person does this automatically. He usually gets ahead in his career, because he is the first to see what is wrong. He always ends up in charge of other people. He is the born inspector, editor, coach or sharpshooter. He is good at any sport involving targetry . . . good at any vocation involving advising. But advice is like salt—it should be used sparingly except when asked for.

The inherently critical person has eyes that slant down from the inner canthus to the outer corner. The eye sits in the socket so that the outer corner is lower than the corner near the nose. (The non-critical eye is the opposite—it slants UPWARD to the outer corner.)

Have you ever cocked your eye to get a better look at something, or to line it up better? (The expression "cocking your eye" comes from cocks—roosters—cocking their eye to better see some moving object.) Some people are built to do this naturally. There is some isomorphic functioning involved in the visual apparatus.

So if you have the sharpshooter's eye and are born critical, save it for when you are paid for it. Then you are praised as the specialist. But off the job, use it only for compliments. Don't make your family and friends afraid of you.

If your youngster comes home from school with four As and one F, FIRST compliment him on the As (and THEN you can ask about the F without making him think that all you do is criticize).

The critical man is a safety engineer, a good job for his build. At work his eagle-eye has probably saved lots of lives in mines, by spotting cracked rafters or the uneven *whirr* of a faulty ventilation fan. But at home, who wants to live with someone who is always pointing out what you have done wrong . . . where you have failed to water the plants. . . . where you have left utensils where the child may hurt herself . . . where you have let your closet get loaded with junk? Not to mention calling you stupid when you burn yourself. Even if he's a millionaire, you are inclined sooner or later to get fed up.

This particular critical man learned his lesson: This is a fine trait used CONSTRUCTIVELY. But when not paid for it . . . talk only of the REDEEMING QUALITY of the person or situation.

So, the next time he saw his wife burn herself, he exclaimed instead, "Oh, I'm so sorry," and went and got some ointment to help her. And she was grateful. He got his inner self, his better self, across. He did not allow a trait to get in the way of expressing his love.

Your traits are a part of you, so you can manage them, just as you can turn your head if you wish. Criticalness is one of the most rewarding traits to express constructively.

In the areas *around* the eyes we find another facet of face language.

Why do women pluck the under part of their eyebrows, and never the upper part? Because: They want to look like actresses. Dramatic actresses have upswept eyebrows. The eyebrow starts where other eyebrows do, but arches high (and ends higher than it started.)

People who have this dramatic inclination naturally, have lively personalities. They can mimic and imitate. Their voice is not monotonous. They can shift easily from one role to another. They make good comedians or comediennes. They have a sense of timing. They know just when to make entrances or exits.

DRAMATIC AND DISCRIMINATING

They are good demonstrators. They can do things for effect
. . . they know how to add the theatrical touch. If they decorate,
there is an easily-recognizable theme or motif—like model air-
planes hung from the ceiling if it's a farewell party, or marine
decorations if it's a bon voyage.

The woman with dramatic eyebrows dresses dramatically.
She is strong on bangle earrings. She may wear a costume, or
some unusual hat like a Sou'wester. Men perk up when she
comes around . . . they take their feet off the table and sit up
straight. Other women are inclined to be jealous of her.

Conversely, the people you know who have very flat eye-

This young woman lacks the hawk nose or Roman nose of the commercial-minded person who is after bargains. She is thinking of the fine meal she will prepare for a dear one. On the daily-life level, traits come out, and her nature is more to help others than it is to bargain.

Face language works with everyone. This young woman has a sense of the dramatic, will talk quite a bit and talk well; she is the opposite of critical, is glad to assist, will stay late or work Saturdays if needed, loves surprises and variety, is open-minded about new subjects but strict enough to see that things get done. She takes her time to get acquainted, but the friends she has accepted are very close friends.

Who is this man climbing up the ladder of success or into your life? Someone who is firm, who will stick out his chin for what he thinks is right, and who will take his obligations seriously. He has a feel for design and structure, likes to have things organized into his own kind of system, and in his own way is generous with all he has to give. Some of this feeling you would get about this person from his photograph or from meeting him; but to know his attributes specifically, you need your face language.

By herself, pensive and concentrating—but how would she be, over a period of time, to know and deal with? From face language, you know she helpful, glad to put in extra time to do her part, is open-minded and trusting . . . also that she is selective about her friends and belongings, and has a sense of protocol and good manners.

What do you notice first about this man? His eyes. He has the sparkling eyes that denote magnetism and liveliness. Also, he has the laugh lines that indicate humor. He is on the thin-skinned side. He has plenty of natural courage. He has quick timing about speaking up about what he feels should not be tolerated. He has a pugnacious trend, and he expresses himself particularly well. He is a good man to have on your side.

Firm, helpful, objective, a bit on the outdoor side—this is what you notice from face language in this young man. Also, that he likes to know why . . . and that he appreciates beauty. Also, he is concerned with details.

brows are less theatrical in their demeanor (see illustration on page 29.) They are aesthetic and want to make an art out of living, but they seek a quieter form of beauty . . . a distillation of the quality or essence of the role or occasion. They want unity. And they need harmony.

If you marry a man with distinctly flat eyebrows, he has much of the aesthete in him. It means much to him if you light the candles for dinner, and if the candles match the drapes. He takes music or some form of art very seriously. Discord or disorder makes him want to go some other place geographically, seeking the beautiful harmonious atmosphere he craves. If there are diapers and dirty dishes around, it's a real tribute to your marriage if he doesn't desert you.

So fundamental is face language, that our native tongue is filled with face language expressions. Acting what others consider "high-brow" comes from raising your eyebrows (or being born that way.)

Remember manners and protocol when dealing with anyone whose eyebrows are perched higher on the forehead than most people's. The man or woman with high eyebrows is offended if you barge in without knocking. Until you are well acquainted, call him or her "Mr." or "Mrs." Show that you understand manners, and that you respect privacy . . . and that you have good taste. Do not expect such a person to open the conversation. Remember, it is up to you to take the lead. Make small talk. Act friendly, but not fresh. Then compliment as you get the opportunity, such as noting what a beautiful picture the hosts have on the wall. FINALLY you can get around to talking about more personal things, such as how long they have known the hostess.

The persons with high eyebrows are strong on being introduced . . . and going through channels. But they may be very warm-hearted (which is another trait), and they can be your very closest and truest friends once they have accepted you. With them, the bars are either clear up or clear down—there is no half way.

(If you yourself happen to be on the high eyebrow side, remember: It is always up to YOU to open the conversation with new individuals, and show them in a friendly way that you have noticed them—or, they will think you are arrogant, or that you think you are better than they are!)

Conversely, you will notice that individuals whose eyebrows sit down close to the eyes are informal and easy to meet, and seldom stuffy. No one seems a stranger to them. They have an engaging way of acting, on first contact, as if you were a dear old friend they had just run into! Many salesmen are this way —they can make "cold calls" and get an audience. This informal or affable build is a great asset in public relations (see illustration on page 29.)

Take out your folding money and look at a picture of Andrew Jackson, Abraham Lincoln, or George Washington. In pictures of these men you can see the upper eyelid plainly, as it covers the upper part of the eyeball.

When you can look in over the eye somewhat and see much of the upper eyelid—when the upper eyelid is well exposed—you are dealing with a person who takes direct action, like Jackson and Lincoln and Washington did. If a battle had

Momentary expressions can be of value. The laugh lines at the outer corners of the eyes show here's a person with a sense of humor, with whom you can kid and joke. Upturned lips are the cue to an optimistic bent. The bright eyes show magnetism and an interest in life.

If you pay attention to the face language beyond the momentary smile, you can anticipate that this charming and generous woman is selective and choosy of her friends and belongings. She leans the direction of good taste, and takes her time to get acquainted. But once she does make a selection, she and her friends are very close.

Warm, affectionate, emotional—that is what the large eyes indicate, especially the large proportion of iris. However intelligent or intellectual, such an person is inclined to make her decisions with her heart instead of her head. Here family and her friends mean a lot to her. She needs to be near them geographically, and to break bread with them. She has a lot of love to give, and she needs a lot of love. She will brighten to your smile or be upset by your frown.

Photos by H. Goodson

This young woman has a flare for the dramatic. She can add the theatrical touch and bring things to life. She has a sense of timing, and can make effective entrances and exits. She can mimic and imitate. She will dress dramatically, and knows how to use jewelry or accessories for effect. Everyone perks up when she comes around. And she loves drama. Her decorating and designing will have a definite motif. In her writing she will have a gift for narrative.

47

LOW ANALYTICALNESS

to be fought, they got it over with. They did not sit on situations and hatch them. They did something about them, at once, even if it seemed ruthless. If you asked a direct question, you got a direct answer.

Now, look at the picture of Alexander Hamilton on some more of your folding money. You cannot see his upper eyelid —it is covered by a fold that is the hallmark of the person who has become very analytical (or who was born that way.) The man who figured out the Treasury Department for our nation so well that it is still going strong with few changes in almost two centuries was great at analyzing and figuring out relationships and ultimate ramifications.

If your employer is built this way, always tell him "why" before you make a request about anything new. (And don't expect any quick answers—he will probably answer your question with another question . . . he will not say "yes" or "no" or "maybe" until he knows all about it.)

If your husband has the analytical build, don't just ask him out of the blue to bring home some extra loaves of bread. FIRST, explain about your being on the social club's sandwich committee. Then he'll do it for you—gladly.

If you are selling and your prospect is analytically inclined, don't just say "This product will pay for itself in two years" and then go on to talk about something else. You have to explain WHY it will pay for itself in two years—or you have lost him, right then. His mind cannot progress beyond a point until he knows the why and wherefore, the logic and relationship.

If you are a teacher, watch the eyes of your analytical students (especially in a solid course like mathematics or science.) If their eyes fog up, you have failed to explain a reason (after which omission they cannot proceed.) Don't just say, "You take a Y out of this side of the equation, too." (Explain WHY both sides of the equation have to be treated in a balanced way.)

If your child is analytical, he likes analytical toys. (Watch out, he may take your best clock apart to see what makes it go —or MADE it go prior to his investigation.)

If your wife is analytical and you have been giving her poor company, explain that you have a toothache (or whatever it is) and she will be happy again . . . otherwise she may figure things out by herself, and come out with the wrong answer, thinking you don't love her any more.

With face language, you can know specifically how to approach the other person, each according to his build. Always remember to use it. Remember, too, your own build, and how to steer it best.

A business executive, high on analyticalness, put this knowledge of himself to work. He no longer cross-examined his wife about little things that he was willing to do anyway. When she asked him, "Will you help me move the table, please?," he brightly responded, "Why sure, sweetheart!" She almost fainted. She asked, "Aren't you going to ask me WHY?" He explained that he was going to save his analyticalness for his work and just have fun at home. Was she ever grateful! (not to mention the children.)

If you are extremely analytical and your work doesn't give you a chance to get it out of your system, play chess . . . by mail —then you can take a week to figure out some move if you want, and it won't bother anybody.

Around the persons who are the direct-actionists, rather than analytical, don't bother with the reasons why. They figure you know what you are doing, or that there must be some good reason. And, don't worry—they can cut through and get things done (if they have a question, they'll ASK you, instead of trying to figure it all out silently by themselves.)

You will observe that women with the direct-action build can hold their own with men out in the business world. The direct-action build may not be good for the diagnostician, but it is great for emergencies where what to do is obvious, such as a fire or earthquake. Even in routine situations, there is a place for the direct-actionist—such as in taking off a bandage that has to come off anyway . . . or in collecting a bill, or repossessing a car, where the attitude pays off of, "if it has to happen, let's get it over with, right away!"

Don't fight the way people are built. Keep your own goals, but fit in with the build of other individuals in carrying out your plans and reaching those goals. You will like how well it works.

There was a munitions ship master hauling ammunition and bombs to Viet Nam who learned the whole personological approach (which goes more deeply and completely than the face language pointers included in this volume.) He studied at the Interstate College of Personology, in San Francisco. He reported this experience in using his knowledge:

"Before I learned personology, I used to try to do the old business of 'Come on now, shape up or ship out—you've all got to be the same.' I had found that the old approach of trying to make each person equal to the other guy (in his way of performing) didn't work—and it was very enervating.

"Now knowing personology I discovered that when I got this bunch of 50 or 60 men aboard my freighter . . . this polyglot crew . . . I knew now that the idea was to make all of these fellows work together as a team. But they *are* all different. So after learning personology, I didn't try to make them all act the same.

"So the job became to *get the best out of what each man was capable of giving.*

"And so I didn't badger somebody and try to get him to come up to somebody else. I saw that he had different potentials and aptitudes. And I got the best I could out of him. Not only was it easier on him, but it was a whole lot easier on me, because

I didn't turn in at night and gnash my teeth because I had been unable to do anything with a certain one."

The men appreciated being treated as individuals. They worked 16 days in stormy weather shoring up bombs after a bomb had become loose. Everyone was on a team and they made port safely.

Use your new knowledge of people just as successfully with your crew, be it a whole factory or just one person, your newly-wed bride!

3. LIPS AND LINES

Abraham Lincoln said, "The Dear Lord gave us our face, but we make our own mouth."

The mouth, especially when relaxed, tells a lot about the person with whom you are dealing. If he has tight thin lips, like the illustration on page 59, expect him to be brief and concise. He will talk "like Western Union." He will say volumes in a few words. He will not waste your time. (And you had better not waste his.) You will be more popular with him if you get to the point, and do not waste a lot of words "gassing."

Think of the people you know who have tight, thin lips like a bear trap. Two words, such as "nice breakfast," is a long sentence for them. Unless he is talking on his pet subject, you can anticipate that such an individual will cover the ground fast conversationally. And he will seem anxious to finish and go.

Should you be the bride of Mr. Concise, and go on a honeymoon with him, expect that everything he does will be done briefly and efficiently. Don't be hurt by thinking him curt. He just has that terse, short way of saying and doing things.

If your nurse has tight, thin lips, you can expect her to tear off just enough bandaging, and just enough tape, to cover the wound. She won't waste any material, or any time.

The full lips are not only decorative. In face language they tell you: Here is a generous disposition. She will stay late or work Saturdays to help out, gladly so. She also will be generous with her words, and more voluble. You can expect her to do quite a bit of talking . . . and to be puzzled and upset if you are on the tight-mouthed side.

Beautiful?—of course! But that you could have told before you had read this book. Now you know from your face language that here is someone warm, generous, dramatic —but choosy, not easily pleased . . . and able to evaluate and criticize, plus an excellent vocabulary and a love of words.

The language of the face is so universally noted, that women with tight, thin lips usually fudge liberally with their lipstick. They endeavor to make their lips look larger and more appealing, more outpouring . . . so they appear less businesslike and less concise. But they will still act brief, tight-mouthed and efficient.

In contrast, the full-lipped person (see illustration on page 54) is generous with time, words, and materials. You can expect him or her to stay late, work Saturdays, or help you move. They are generous with all they have to give (they may not have any money left, because of their outpouring disposition, but they will be generous with all they have).

If you are going into the post office and need some extra assistance, go to the window where the most large-lipped clerk is. He likely will spend the time to help you more securely wrap the package, instead of telling you to go home and bring it back.

You can anticipate that the full-lipped person will lean toward the direction of automatically giving. Don't hire him as your credit manager. He will fit more naturally and happily into social welfare.

If you have a full-lipped youngster, teach him or her to be a better manager of time. Say: "Deadlines are your best friends . . . act like you had a plane to catch on a happy trip you had won, all expenses paid!" Train them to have such an attitude of buzzing happily through what they must do. Otherwise they will be slow to get started and slow to finish.

If you have full-lipped employees who spend too much time and wordage preparing reports, tell them: "I want it written briefly, like you would if you were cabling it to Hong Kong at four dollars a word."

55

If your date has full lips and is ready on time, that individual is really interested in you.

If basically your thoughts are pessimistic, your mouth betrays it by drooping at the corners. It becomes a "sour puss." So seldom do you smile at your own mental pictures (or at what you see in front of you) that the muscles which are supposed to lift the corners of the lips in a smile become unused and weak.

The individual with the pessimistic mouth (see illustration on page 56) looks like a person who would be less fun to be around, everything else being equal—and that's pretty liable to

PESSIMISM

be the way it turns out. Others are liable to choose for company someone else who looks like more fun because of the happy mouth with upturned lips at the corners.

NOTE: While this book is written especially to give you cues on the face language you read from the countenance of others, remember *they are getting impressions from you, too.* So if you notice in the mirror that you have accumulated a droopy-lipped, pessimistic expression, work to regain a happy-mouthed appearance. Practice your big million-dollar smile on every mirror you come across. Think smiling. Talk about the pleasant.

Look at the illustration on page 63 for the happy mouth, the badge of the optimist. Indeed, a merry heart makes a cheerful countenance.

So universal is the recognition of this quality, that in drama there have been masks for centuries depicting by contrast the happy upturned lips of the optimistic comedian, and the sad drooping mouth of the tragedian.

When you meet someone, whether they have an optimistic, happy mouth, or a dejected pessimistic mouth, tells you a lot about how pleasant they would be as companions over a period of time.

One instructor in drama who understands face language decides by the mouth who is the winner of a close audition. When two actors read the part equally well, he will select the happy-mouthed one for the cast. The instructor knows that the optimistic candidate will be more good-natured when there are unexpected delays in rehearsals. Watch and you will notice that the person with the upturned lips just naturally expects things to work out all right in the long run . . . (and will do less complaining.)

If you are choosing a hostess or receptionist, pick the applicant who has the happy mouth.

The mouth faithfully reflects the concensus of your thoughts, and your smiles or grimaces. It is one of the most noticeable parts of your visage. It gives automatic expression to deeper and more important parts of your nature.

You yourself are gravitating, when you have a choice, to others with happier, pleasant countenances. And they likewise are choosing, as much as they can, the company of individuals who look like they would be a pleasure to be around. So you owe it to yourself to develop upturned, optimistic lips, if up to the time you read this book you have been a sour-puss. Since your lips reflect the concensus of your mental smiles and frowns, as well as your conscious physical smiles or pouts, this may mean you are going to have to do some mental housecleaning. Think only of the best. Work only for the best. Expect only the best. Do your part to make it happen. You will surprise no one more than yourself as your mouth (and your nature) end up happier. Others will seek you out more . . . and they will find that you are continually, rather than sporadically, your best self.

Generally speaking, vertical lines on the face are linked up with worry or aging, and the horizontal lines are more youthful. This is especially true around the eyes.

Think of someone you know who has vertical worry-lines between the eyebrows. That person is fussy and exacting. He cuts the firewood off to the 1/16th of an inch. He's a nit-picker. He's forever going back and double-checking. He's a perfectionist. (See the illustration on page 67.) Not too much fun to be with on a honeymoon, as far as this trait goes. If he's your

CONCISE

boss, to click with him have things exactly as he wants, down
to the dot.

Wanting to make sure that things are perfect, the possessor
of worry-lines keeps thinking about something he has done
until he doubts himself. The exacting operator of a welding
shop arrives home at the end of the day and gets to thinking
about what he has done—he begins to worry about whether he
really locked the front door when he left the shop. Finally he
calls up the cafe owner across the street from his shop. He asks
his restaurant friend to go across the street and make sure he

locked the door! (Almost always, he HAS locked it.)

The exacting office worker opens up the envelope he just sealed, to end his doubts as to whether he signed the enclosed check.

The exacting mother telephones the society editor an additional time to ask the writer if she got her daughter's middle name spelled just right after all, in the wedding story.

If your husband (or wife) has worry lines, and asks you to be at the meeting place for lunch at 12:00 noon, be there at *12* —not at 11:35 or 12:15. It's a cheap way to keep such a person happy. (If you want to please someone, fit in with their traits, instead of fighting their build—just as you do not resent having to buy a particular kind of battery for your transistor radio instead of another size . . . be scientific with people, just as you are with other things on earth.)

One exacting funeral director would fire any office employee who let the phone ring three times before answering it. Before he was told about his over-exacting nature, this mortician would fuss around so much, double-checking the flowers and cards and arrangements, that he would be laid up for a few days after a large funeral. After he was counseled personologically, he only *single*-checked, at the time . . . and lost in a year the long worry line which had indented his lower forehead between the eyebrows.

Perhaps in a life-and-death situation, the double-checking which an exacting person does may be valuable—such as in setting off a charge of dynamite . . . or in cutting the Hope diamond (where great stakes exist and there is plenty of time.) But for better functioning in the ordinary situations of life, use this procedure and get rid of the worry line or worry lines: *just be careful in the first place, and then refuse to go back over it again.* Do not double-check mentally or physically. Just handle things once. Just "chew your cabbage once." No post-mortems.

The student pilot who buzzes the field a dozen times before he finally thinks everything is JUST right to set his plane down on the landing strip builds up more vacillation than he does skill. (Not to mention the worry lines he may give his instructor!)

To shake off worry lines, don't scotch tape them out of your brow at night and expect them to disappear for keeps while you are sleeping. Remember instead, mentally as well as physically, to do no "remakes." Carefully read the fine print *before* you sign the contract. Have your prospective life partner personologized before getting engaged. Never dwell on happenings long since carried out, such as whether you moved to the right town or took the right job.

Most likely, if you have worry lines, you developed them from the best of intentions. You built fussiness as a crutch to avoid getting into any more hot water into which you had been plunged previously by carelessness or impetuousness. But if you keep doubting yourself and running back and forth double-checking, you require twice as much time. By handling things just once, you not only lose your worry lines, but you have twice as much time left over to do things you want.

Know, too, that you are going to handle things only once, so it "had better be GOOD." As you take pains to do things right in the first place, you develop more faith in yourself. When taking an address down over the phone, tell the caller, "I want this to be sure to reach you—how do you spell that, please, and what is the zip code?" Then you can dismiss it from your mind.

Keeping your youthfulness of approach also keeps your youthfulness of visage. You do a face-lifting job, so to speak, on the inside as well as on the outside . . . one that lasts, and brings along lots of fringe benefits.

While you are getting rid of your worry lines, you discover usually that there are reasonable precautions already set up or required in most areas of activity, if you will pay attention to them. No need later to double-check yourself. The bookkeeper balances across and up and down the columns. The linotypist's accuracy is checked by the proofreader. The carpenter breeds carefulness in his apprentice by telling him, "Measure twice and cut once."

So now you know what to do to get rid of your own worry lines if you possess them—as well as how to anticipate and fit in with associates who bear this well-intentioned but heavy badge of fussiness.

Now for happy lines:

In contrast with the vertical worry lines you may find between the eyebrows of the fussy person, some people have happy, sunny lines which fan out from the outer corner of each eye. These "laugh lines" indicate an appreciation of the funny side of things. (See the illustration on page 102.)

You can kid someone who has laugh lines. But if you try to kid somebody who has no laugh lines, it goes over like a lead balloon. Think of the people you know with laugh lines, and they all possess a good sense of humor. They can even laugh at themselves. They can see the ridiculous side of a situation, even such as changing a tire in the rain.

All successful salesmen, ministers and priests have these laugh lines. Humor is the lubricant of daily affairs. Also, when

OPTIMISM

you are traveling, it is the universal language. You know at whom to smile when you explain, "Ich bin Amerikaner," or "Yo soy Americano."

Marriage is a lot easier if you have picked a partner with a good sense of humor. Your own sense of humor not only can keep up your own morale, but it can brighten the day for those around you. If you look in the mirror and see you lack laugh lines, build them. This you do by entering your daily situations good-humoredly, the way crowds do when they pour into a ball game, expecting to have a good time regardless of who wins.

Also build humor by thinking and talking of the pleasant. Make conversation around the most pleasant thing in sight, or the most pleasant thing that happened on your last trip. Then the tone of the conversation is up to talking about the funniest things you have heard or experienced lately.

Making at least one person a day smile builds up your humor. Similarly, make at least one person a week laugh out loud—to do this, you have to be in a good-humored mood yourself. Just like you cannot hand someone a pencil unless you have a pencil, you cannot hand someone humor unless you feel good-humored yourself. So if you start building laugh lines, you will find you are in for a revolution in your ways of thinking, and of talking.

Incidentally, people who express themselves vigorously by word of mouth develop decided lines which run from the edge of the nose to the edge of the mouth. You will notice these lines on attorneys, teachers, actors and others who say things like they mean them, with a great deal of unction . . . crunching the muscles around the mouth so that the vigor helps produce the line that runs from the edge of the mouth up to the edge of the nostrils. These lines always indicate decided expression orally —if you are this way, people remember what you say; they could tell you your own words a week later.

You may be interested to know that the fine lines which fan out from the INNER corners of the eyes, out over the cheek bones, indicate rhetoric, or a feeling for the exact word and the flow of words. The possessor has a keen feel for the right word, which to him is like a hole-in-one in golf—it just fills the bill. He also has a feeling for the wrong word and is irritated by it (watch your grammar!). Usually he (or she) will have quite a

THIN SKINNED (indoor build)
(plus GENEROSITY)

vocabulary, too. These fine lines are not to be confused with puffiness or bagginess under the eyes.

If you are a secretary or a journalist and have copious rhetoric lines fanning out over the cheekbone from the inner corners of the eyes, there is no use trying to rub them out with cold cream. They won't go. They indicate your keen appreciation of words. So enjoy them. And remember, to everyone who knows face language, they are a badge of keen appreciation of words and love of a well turned phrase.

4. FLEETING EXPRESSIONS

When mother gets a glint in her eye and an edge on her voice, Junior knows that she means business and that he'd better stop giving her trouble and do what she says. When your wife bursts out crying and sobs on your shoulder, you know she is eating her heart out about something. When the other driver sets his jaw and juts his chin out in front, you know you'd better give him the right-of-way.

If you miss such obvious indications given by the face language of other people, you deserve everything that happens to you.

In high-voltage moments of rage, joy, grief or pain, the facial indications are correspondingly high-voltage, due to the way your physical mechanism is all hooked up together. It would be pretty hard for you to miss such high-voltage indications. But at turning points in smaller episodes of life, you will need to be more alert to know what the other person's inclination is at the moment. There are such indications.

If you are selling, and the other person hardens the lower eyelid and sets it rigidly—that is the place where you have lost him and he has determined not to buy.

When the other individual's eyes start wandering around the room, or he begins to look at his watch, he has lost interest.

When the other person's eyes go dull, you have said something he does not understand according to his build, or which does not appeal to him.

When your child begins to whine or be irritable, he is in need of some physical attention (probably food or rest.) When

EXACTING AND ANALYTICAL

The basic personality is abiding. Momentary expressions can change. The actor knows how to turn these expressions on and off. They are worth watching, as obvious cues of the current mood. Here's a relaxed, friendly mood, smiling, with pleasant eyes. The indications of present mood give you obvious signals in the present-moment situation or conversation. If you overlook them, you have only yourself to blame.

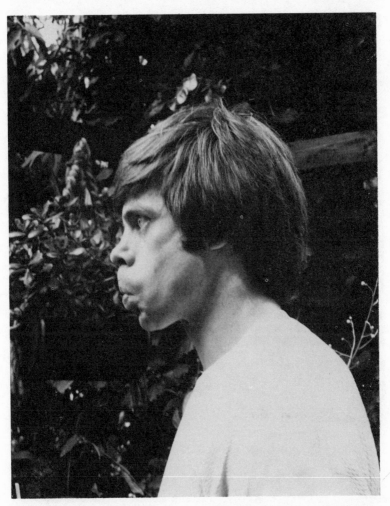

Well, well! What kind of expression is this? Not the ordinarily, for sure. Is he showing off, or is he about to explode? Actually, it's an actor just clowning. Keep a list of expressions you encounter in people you meet during the day, and you will find they vary not too much, nor are they puzzling. The expression of the moment is a valuable indicator. But the hot buttons to press to reach the basic nature beneath, are always available. You will notice that his photograph shows the same traits as the picture facing it (notably the helpfulness and the friendliness and sense of humor . . . these causal traits are what will triump in the long run).

Fortunately, you don't often have to decipher a momentary expression as puzzling as the grimace of this actor. But if you will refer to his picture on the opposite page, you will see he still has the same basic disposition to deal with—rather mild or small ego, rich love of words, plenty of feeling, underlying friendliness, and a trend toward the esthetic and artistic.

70

What's the momentary expression here? Anyone would know it's of friendly, alert interest. You know that as far as his mood of the moment goes, he could be expected to pay attention and to be cooperative.

your child begins to frown or fuss or fidget, odds are that the bathroom facilities are needed.

From now on, you will be more alert to such cues, and will handle situations more quickly and successfully. When a hurt look comes in the other person's eyes, you are given a cue about something important to him. Ask him what he feels bad about (or if you already know that it is something you have done, apologize.)

The other person's frown is an indication of disagreement or puzzlement.

When the other individual looks like he wants to talk, stop talking and listen. If you wait until the other person gets red with anger before you pay attention, then you have only yourself to blame for how you have "blown it."

Some of the most important communications are nonverbal, such as a blush, a twinkle in the eye, or a wink. ("Your lips say 'No, No,' but it's 'Yes, Yes' in your eyes," as the song goes.)

Conversely, if your boss is glassy-eyed and frowning the morning you planned to ask him for a raise, postpone it until you find him in a better mood (or you may get fired instead!).

There is so very much that can be told without words (in fact sometimes words get in the way—actions speak louder than words.) A man can be insolent to his superior without saying a word . . . or he can be quite gentle and tender, helping some poor old crippled lady with her crutches out of a cab, without saying a word.

Read this unspoken language, and put to use what you read. You will get to your goals faster and more smoothly.

MAGNETISM (Charm)

And the other person will be grateful, or more cooperative—
or both.

My wife is very good at gauging people on initial contact.
She has a 100% record on spotting women who are two-timing
their husbands. She has never missed on recognizing a homo-
sexual.

She says that married women who are having sex with
someone other than their husband have a haughty, rather de-
fiant attitude . . . much as if to say, "Who are you . . . and how
are you going to stop me, or prove anything?" (Girls who are

73

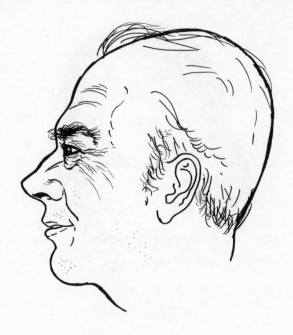

RHETORIC (also Humor)

having sex outside of wedlock have somewhat of the same hard attitude but it is mixed more with an uneasiness, and very often with melancholy, unhappy eyes.)

There are many variations of male homosexuals. The most obvious to spot is the man who walks and talks in a rather prissy way. He does not set his foot down heavily. He does not stomp along. He uses his hands much like a woman, with dainty gestures. His voice pattern is much like a woman's (usually with excellent diction and precise enunciation, and easily recognized over the telephone). He will giggle much like a woman or girl.

His conversation is often like a woman, such as "Oh, I'm delighted . . . I've just found the right color dinner candles to match the curtains!"

Such behavior and characteristics about extreme homosexuals are so obvious that when their nature becomes apparent, you kick yourself for not having spotted it at first. You could have. The signals were plainly out.

5. THE CLOUDED BROW

No one is born with a clouded brow. But some individuals build it up by getting hung up on details. They hate details—but like the bird hypnotized by the snake, they can't get away from paying great attention to trivia. They develop a knotted brow (see illustration on page 83.) This indicates detail concern. Some even build up a ledge clear across the lower forehead, right above the eyebrows—their way of going at things extends beyond detail concern into outright methodicalness.

When you are dealing with anyone possessing detail concern, remember that he is observant of everything. He will notice whether anything has been moved a half inch to the right, or a half inch to the left. He could find anything in his room in the dark, if it hasn't been moved by someone.

This does *not* mean that he LIKES details. He will tell you that he does indeed hate them. But they have come to occupy a place on his horizon of observation that is out of all proportion to their significance. They upset him more than big things—a reminder of the saying that we never stumble over a mountain, always over a rock or a twig. He can rise to big occasions—they force him to a breakthrough.

You can safely mention to the detail-ridden man that he

is gallant to his wife if she has survived totaling the car in a wreck—but heaven help her if she has merely lost the keys in ordinary everyday events! (that really puts him in a bad mood).

Detail concern is usually developed in a well-intentioned way, trying to do a better job—but it is a crutch, nevertheless, built up in trying to protect the person from difficulties due to other traits, such as an easy-going nature. A far better way to do a good job, rather than approaching from the viewpoint of details, is to plan to do a thorough job—and to take care of the details as they unfold. One should not build his schedule around having noticed he needs a shoe shine or that he has run out of postage stamps. When you are around the person high on detail concern, don't upset him by failing to take care of details.

If your husband is high on detail, and he mentions to you, "This shirt needs a button sewed on it," right away fast sew that button! (And put a note in his pocket saying, "I'm so glad I have YOU to sew a button for. Little things mean a lot to him.

If you are a salesman and you notice your customer is high on detail, make sure everything in your demonstration kit works well. He frowns if something of yours has broken, or if you can't locate something you want to show him. It is very hard for him to see the forest for the trees, so to speak.

If your employer is heavy on detail, an easy way to please him is to follow quickly his suggestions about detail. If he has remarked, "You ought to put a new ribbon in that typewriter," do it right away . . . that's the first thing to do to please him . . . and show him a sample of the new typing, to show him how well his idea worked out. This is his idea of cooperation. When time comes for Christmas bonuses, he's likely to give you a large one—you are HIS kind of employee. Handling details well makes him happier than if you had brought in a new customer.

To your boss (or to your husband, if he is detail concerned) don't too often bring up little details you haven't taken care of, which sound to him like problems. He frowns and studies . . . and dwells on the subject . . . he instructs you how to handle it, and how not to let it happen again. It is better to concentrate on showing him what has been done well. He already has enough self-inflicted troubles of his own by making mountains out of mole hills. He may have a wonderful new car, but be upset and unhappy with the whole car because one door-latch needs fixing. The whole first day of his vacation trip is spoiled because the lid came off one jar in the picnic-food carrier and spilled pickle juice on the bottom.

If your husband is heavy on detail, coach the children to keep their bicycles out of the driveway. And see to it that you have the whole newspaper ready for him to read—not just one section.

I have helped a great many detail-concerned salesmen to make more money, simply by telling them to start out each day by doing things that will count, before they even open their mail . . . and to save for after 3 p.m. the trivia which a 12-year-old could do. This keeps up their momentum, and avoids their occupying themselves with unimportant details instead of getting out on the firing line. (Try this yourself, if you are high on detail concern—besides achieving more, you will have more carefree enjoyment in life, as you show you still can see the town in spite of the houses, as it were . . . and that little things cannot get your goat, or set the SEQUENCE of what you do.)

And you are liable to be more popular with those who deal closely with you. If your wife has lost some of your income tax records, while they are being found comfort her instead of lecturing her. Tell her, "Don't feel bad, honey . . . that could happen to anyone . . . it'll be okay."

It may take quite a while to erase the physical indicator for detail concern (hyperplasia of the superciliary arch) but right away you will begin to reap the benefits.

When the indicators for detail concern are more than the two protrusions shown in the illustration on page 67, and instead have become a continuous ledge across the lower part of the forehead, you can expect that person to be *methodical.* He

LOW TOLERANCE

will want to do things according to a system . . . to get organized. He may be original or unconventional so that his system may not seem like a system to anyone else, but it is to him. He will have the same procedure or routine in what he does when he first gets up—he will hang his towel just the same way . . . his shaving and shoeshining will always be in the same order.

Fit in with what Mr. Methodical is used to. Put his socks always in the same drawer, so he never screams at you when he can't find them in the accustomed place. Have an extra bottle of lotion behind the usual one, so when the usual one runs out, the next one is already there. And around Mr. Methodical, give him extra credit if he makes love to you differently or creatively. Ordinarily, you know before he does, what he is going to do— because you have so often observed his pattern. Probably he's pretty certain to make love on Saturday night, because on Sunday he can sleep late! If he does make love to you imaginatively, that's real love, in his case.

NOTE: The worry lines described in the section on face lines, also add to the clouded or worried expression of the brows. If the person with whom you're dealing has the vertical furrows of exactingness as well as the ledge of detail concern, then he's fussy as well as inclined to focus on details. Follow the instructions all the more assiduously for both traits. At least you know what you are up against! Forewarned is fore-armed.

6. THIN-SKINNED OR THICK-SKINNED?

You don't need to shout at anyone who has fine, porcelain-like skin and "baby hair." They are on the sensitive side physically. Expect them to act thin-skinned. Use your gentleness and finesse around them. Show you have some subtlety. They like refinement. Their tastes are expensive . . . they like quality instead of quantity.

If your wife is built this way, treat her like a princess. Her idea of roughing it is still to have hot and cold running water, so be careful where you take her in the mountains. In buying gifts for her, remember she would rather have a quarter ounce of fine perfume than a whole quart of cologne. In taking her out to dine, you will get more appreciation from her if you save up the money and take her once to a fine restaurant, than if you take her six times to a drive-in. Be careful, too, of the language you use around her—she shrinks at coarseness.

The man with the thin-skinned build and silky hair has more gentleness. He will have a quieter laugh, and never a bellowing belly laugh. Due to other traits, he may be just as

81

courageous or belligerent as anyone else, but always he will have the finer, more velvety mannerism in carrying out his actions. He is more silken and less like burlap.

The rougher, robust, "polar bear" kind of man has coarser hair and skin. His features are less finely chiseled. He is hearty and vigorous in his way of functioning. You can hear his laughter or his shout a half block away. So to speak, he is wired for 220-volts instead of 110-volts. He likes fresh air and to be close to nature . . . he loves the out-of-doors. He can dish it out, and he can take it. Depending upon other traits, his language will be more direct, with plainer, short words. He is basic and primal.

Women usually are more on the thin-skinned, fine-haired side, in their build. But some of them have rough textures like "Tugboat Annie"—they are rough and hearty and direct, love vigorous experience with nature, can "take it" physically, and should be spoken to plainly instead of by subtle hints. Their hair seldom or never needs a permanent . . . if it happens to be curly, it will have its own permanent for keeps. One woman I know who is built this way has a hobby of deep-sea fishing, and enjoys it. She comes of conquistador lineage.

A housing executive with training in personology and a knack at understanding face language, won a government citation for her skill in assigning individuals to housing units where they fitted together harmoniously. She put the thin-skinned in one building, where together they would maintain a quiet, refined atmosphere. She put the rough-hewn applicants in another building, where (together) they could be as rough or noisy as they wanted and it would bother no one.

Incidentally, you can please thin-skinned people more

with the more delicate colors and pastels. The rougher-textured like vigorous basic colors.

Some people are soft and wishy-washy. Some are hard as nails. This is evidenced by whether their flesh is soft and droopy.

The soft person also has more of a whining voice. When pronounced, it can be noticed even over the telephone. The soft individuals hate to have to follow through. Keep checking up on them to see they do what they have promised.

The flesh of the soft person hangs somewhat from the

DETAIL CONCERN

This young husband and father is sharp, will be right on top of everything, but at the same time craves beauty and harmony, and wants to make an art out of living. He has a firm disposition, is observant of every detail, and likes to know the reasons behind what he does. He likes travel and the out-of-doors.

The young wife and mother has a spiritual quality about her, and is generous to a fault and is on the warm and affectionate and sympathetic side. But also she strongly resents being pushed to do something. She wants things in good taste, and she values her privacy.

The 19-months-old daughter is a child who needs to learn a step at a time from the very beginning, and to have a good foundation . . . after she has caught on to something and feels familiar with it, she can speed up. She is on the serious-minded side and should have things explained to her but with a loving voice.

Face language opens up a whole new world for you. You can anticipate a good deal from photographs of people you are going to meet. If you have been reading this book carefully, you will see that this man is concise and brief, but optimistic and pleasant to be with. He has lots of humor and is at home with words; he expresses himself well orally. He is analytical and does things more quickly for you if you explain "why" it needs to be done before you make the request. He has the sharpshooter's critical eye and will give you good advice, if asked for. He has the worry lines of exactingness and will want things just so . . . you will please a man like this if you are on time.

Most people only say when seeing a couple like this, "What a handsome pair!" But if you know face language, you see deeper, and even look ahead. The bride has lots of self-confidence. She will want to move ahead in life in a big way, and think in big terms. She is an idealist and a romanticist. She will need variety and change, and will love to travel. She likes surprises. Everything for her should be gift-wrapped. She is broad-minded but ladylike, and needs privacy and must have everything in good taste. She has enthusiasm and sparkle and much energy. She is willing to do her part, but she has the eye of the adviser and coach and will need to remember not to give suggestions or reminders to her husband unless he asks.

The bridegroom is an expanding personality, still anxious to prove himself and move ahead. He loves beauty and must have harmony, and is in many ways a perfectionist. He has, too, a rough-hewn, vigorous side to his nature, and enough impatience to keep things moving. He is a competitor. He is restless and adventurous and can set quite a pace for anyone to follow. He has plenty of comprehension and initiative. This couple has plenty in common to make a good marriage if they understand each other as individuals.

Handsome hair and beard are decorative. But you are going to deal with the personality, individuality, native qualities of the person, more than with hirsute adornment. If you have a grasp of face language, you appreciate that here is a man who can get his way with people, and who must have his own way and run his own show. He is analytical and likes to understand reasons and relationships, and is a natural analyst. The rhetoric lines fanning out from the inner corners of his eyes are exceptional, indicating writing and speaking ability and unusual vocabulary. He has authoritativeness balanced with humor, has more than his share of magnetism and charm, and has the perfectionist indications for wanting this just so . . . besides which he possesses a plenty of self-confidence and thoroughness. He's a bit on the broad-minded side, and has lots of ideas and lots of push, pride in his appearance, and a love of the artistic and creative.

86

What would this man be like to go shopping with? Use your face language, and then you can anticipate that he would be critical about what would be purchased—and also might be giving some extra advice . . . that he takes a generally serious attitude, but nevertheless enjoys kidding and can be kidded; that he likes to make an adventure out of the trip . . . that he has quite a vocabulary and enjoys the exact word and the well-turned phrase . . . that he is helpful and would volunteer to carry your packages (and doesn't haggle over money . . . and that he loves harmony and beauty and the gracious extras.

cheek or chin or arms. The hard person looks more firm and the face flesh may seem a bit puffed out. The hard person walks with a more vigorous step—you are inclined to get out of his way if he comes toward you on the sidewalk. You will find hard people exactly where you would expect them—in situations requiring toughness: miners, lumberjacks, combat soldiers . . . and, bill collectors.

Whereas the soft individual easily agrees with you, because that is less bother than disagreeing, the hard person is hard to make a dent on. But when you have convinced him, he stays put—and his action is vigorous. You do not have to call him up a day later to see if he still means it.

Many teenagers, especially boys, have gotten hard and unresponsive. You have to get their attention directly and forcibly, for anything to register. What you tell them, you had better have them tell back to you, to make sure it got through and that they intend to do something about it. The hard person is genuine. If you can get them to smile, they mean it. They like to work with hard materials.

Whereas the soft person wants a lot of cushions around, the hard individual likes simple, more durable furniture, and less of it.

Getting a response out of a hard person may seem like pounding on a rock with a sledgehammer. You have to keep pounding away . . . but finally, when it does split, it splits wide open.

When the hard person to whom you are trying to sell something SEEMS responsive but says nothing (and is not belligerent) do not be discouraged, but keep up your presentation. He may very well be on your side and just listening and thinking it out.

When the hard individual does respond, his response is complete and vigorous. If he gives you a hug and you are soft, watch out: he may crack a rib or two, or take your breath away!

NOTE: You can always talk directly to any trait you notice about the other individual. But there are people who have one trait amplifying another, such as a thick-skinned, rough-hewn person also being tough and hard, in which case he will seem even more durable and insensitive. Or, some finely-textured person may have allowed himself or herself to have gotten soft and draggy, in which case the sensitivity is exaggerated, and the individual may be horrified at the thought of a cold shower, or clam up sensitively at something you have said where you wonder, "Now, what in the world have I said wrong?" So when one trait boosts up the effect of another, you have the challenge of being doubly alert to click properly with that particular human being.

7. PROPORTIONS

Nature builds in harmony. The round-faced person is usually round elsewhere, too. The square-faced person is more liable to be square-shouldered.

Dr. William Sheldon has done a great deal of research on individuals' proportions of basic cells. He has found that the round, roly-poly "endomorph" is consistently more jovial, jolly and gregarious. Think of the round-faced men or women you know, and this is generally true. They are the born hosts and politicians. They are great at entertaining and at creature comforts. They have a knack at food and shelter. They are more likely to be the gourmets. They are never broke, because that might mean they would miss a meal. They make the most of everything. They set up housekeeping wherever they go. At the ball game they are organized with blankets and refreshments they have brought along. They seldom alienate their support . . . they can have all sides of the family tribe behind them— or if they are in politics, they can have groups of Democrats and Republicans supporting them.

The moon-faced, conserving individual hates to see anything go to waste. He will eat it instead . . . so he is liable to get round below as well as above. He likes to make use of

CONSERVATION
(plus Thin-Skinned)

leftovers (some round-face in a past generation doubtless was the inventor of hash). Also he combines errands, to save extra expenditure of time and gasoline. The round-faced man or woman is more naturally domestic. The home is the hub of life for such a person.

In contrast, the square-faced, bone and muscle men build and dig and fight, and change the face of the earth. They are more mesomorphic, with more inclination to get wrapped up in their careers and projects, and miss meals and neglect the calls of nature.

CONSTRUCTION
(plus Outdoor-Build)

If you marry a square-faced woman, you can anticipate that she will be less jovial and jolly, more of the doer and less of the enjoyer. She likes projects, and soon runs out of them inside the house . . . she will find work outside, or at least run the PTA. She would be "climbing the walls" if kept cooped up. She is more the homemaker than she is the housekeeper— maintenance routine (the same old dishes and laundry-sorting) bores her. If this is the way your wife is built, take her out to dinner at least once a week—and give her some moral support in expressing her talents outside in some way, beyond the housekeeping routine.

Observe and you will notice that individuals relatively wide between the eyes take a more philosophical, broader view on life. They are more easy-going.

This is not a matter of inches or pounds, but of relative placement. Think of anyone you know who is noticeably wide between the eyes, and you realize *that* individual is one who puts up with a lot before ever "blowing his stack."

THICK SKINNED
(plus High Tolerance)

The silky "baby" hair and fine skin tip you off that this young lady is on the fine-textured side, physically sensitive and with expensive tastes . . . and that she will lean more toward refinement. Her face is mobile and elastic, with flesh neither soft nor hard—on acquaintance she will prove to be neither soft-and-wishy-washy nor tough and unresponsive, but will rather prove to be flexible and enthusiastic.

There is a relation between structure and function, isomorphically. Things seem further off, and not so pressing, to the man or woman broad between the eyes. It isn't late enough yet. Or it isn't bad enough. They can tolerate a lot. But correspondingly, they are liable to let situations build up. And very often they are late.

If your wife is broad between the eyes, chances are she is good-natured, but late with breakfast.

If your teen-ager is broad between the eyes, you are used to getting notices from his teachers that he "does not apply himself." He is inclined to put off writing his report until the night before it is due. He needs checking up on, or he may go swimming when he should be doing his homework. In getting ready for life, he can profit by some teaching along the lines of performing instead of intending . . . keeping ahead of schedule . . . and that anything worth doing is worth doing well.

Conversely, the people noticeably close between the eyes take a closer view on things. They are harder to please, and more the perfectionists. They are the supervisors, the precision workers, highly conscientious. They deserve credit if they never get ulcers, for by nature their inclination is to try to carry the whole world on their shoulders. (They worry more about whether their parent is getting their vitamins than the parent does.)

Look at your wife. If she is close between the eyes, she does a beautiful job, but she is hard to please. She is so very concerned about everything. If you are going to be late getting home, call her up and let her know. (And never dance twice in a row with some other woman or you will upset her and make her act jealous . . . and she won't wait until she gets home to tell you about it, either.)

Your statements around the close-eyed person had better be acccurate, and not broad or sweeping. If you are choosing an auditor, hire the one close between the eyes. If you are selecting somebody to do public relations, hire the more broad-minded, good-natured individual, wide between the eyes.

What's most strikingly different about the person with whom you are dealing is what you want to notice. It is the extremes which make the salt and pepper of the personality . . . and which are most easily noticed. If the person is about average in the quality considered, then that factor makes little difference—shift your attention to one of the other characteristics described in this volume, and you will soon notice plenty of qualities which are distinct about the person (and easily visible.)

8. SOME TIPS FROM ARISTOTLE

Aristotle, the father of science, said the Greeks of his time had two systems of noticing a person's natural individuality from his structure. He used one quite successfully in picking generals for his pupil Alexander the Great.

Aristotle suggested that the structure/function approach be carried further, isolating as many human traits as possible connected with native build. He recommended noticing what certain persons have in common in their inherent traits and tendencies—and then ascertaining the physical concomitant. Today we would call that "behavioral genetics" in one of its applications.

The suggestion by Aristotle has been carried out systematically by the Interstate College of Personology. Using a base population of 1,050 northern California and Oregon adults, and utilizing twentieth century scientific methodology, 68 human structure/function relationships have been indicated as statistically significant at the one percent level. Some of this knowledge easily adaptable in daily life has been transmitted to you in this book, for your enjoyment and benefit.

From an earlier section of this volume, you are already acquainted with one valuable segment of Aristotle's findings:

that people built rough, rugged and hearty are inclined to act rough, rugged and hearty . . . and that people built more thin-skinned and delicate are inclined to act thin-skinned and delicate.

A couple more of Aristotle's findings have stood the test of statistical correlation, and I relay them to you as knowledge useful and valuable in your daily life.

Aristotle noticed that broad-faced living creatures have more audacity, more sureness of themselves . . . and will more quickly act more thoroughly and more courageously. They are

CONSTRUCTION (career-minded)
(plus Low Tolerance)

more the Churchill and less the Chamberlain. By nature they easily think in big terms. They seldom "chicken out." When the going gets tough, they get tough. They have lots of self-confidence . . . they figure that "they can do it," if they turn their mind to it. They have lots of inner strength and a high opinion of their own ability. They naturally take over. (See illustration on page 111 for this broad-faced build . . . which, like other personological indications, is a PROPORTION, not a matter of inches or pounds.) There is a saying along this line which goes, "It's not the size of the dog in the fight. It's the size of the fight in the dog!"

How do you apply this knowledge to your daily events? Don't start something with the broad-faced, self-confident person that you can't finish. He's a real tiger, not a paper tiger.

These qualities, which are really based on cell proportions, apply to children, too. Your broad-faced child acts like an adult, as far as self-confidence goes. He is liable to try to advise YOU, or tell you what to do (and to inform you about what he is going to do, and what he is NOT going to do!)

Challenges look pretty small to the self-confident youngster. I recall one self-confident boy, age 8, who (on his own) used to go down to the fire-house and ride on the fire truck, on practice runs. The firemen were delighted with the self-confident exuberance of the small lad.

If your husband has broad self-confidence, he will wear the pants. You do not need to worry about beating his ego down. You will not need to call the boss to make excuses for him— he will call the boss himself if there's anything to tell him, and it won't be said as an excuse, but just as a statement, if something has turned up and he's not coming to work that day. He

MELANCHOLY

may have other traits so that he is not a show-off, but he still makes the final decisions in your family. He has a strong shoulder for you to lean on.

The wife with broad self-confidence has to watch out or she just naturally appears to take over. Sooner or later that will backfire. There can only be one skipper on the ship. If you are a wife and are built broad-faced, take it easy—don't get into the mother role. Don't seem to be telling your husband how to drive . . . when with him, be a success of your gender ("you Jane, he Tarzan.") Be the cheerleader instead of the quarter-

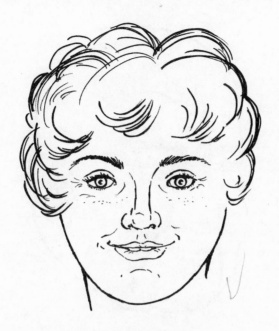

CONSERVING (domestic) (also tolerant)

back. Pat his cheek. Wool his hair. Scrub his back. And you will find him bringing you what you want, on a platter. But stay out of the mother role. Save that for your children. And use your leadership to run the Parent Teachers Association . . . throw your weight around on "your own 10 acres." But whenever you go on the mutual territory with your husband, wear something to remind you of your sweetheart role there . . . eye-shadow, a ribbon around your hair, high heels, a beauty mark on your cheek . . . or a lace handkerchief or a frilly blouse. It simply works better, to be biological on the biological acreage. Do this

HUMOR

consistently, in spirit as well as letter, freely playing your feminine cards on the man-and-woman mutual territory, and you will never see the inside of a divorce court. (Remember, too, that as big and strong as your man is, he is only human—if he is cut, he will bleed; he has his ups and downs, and can stand having a cheerleader, a comforter, someone who is fun and has faith in him and builds him up, instead of instructing him.)

Now consider the narrow-faced individuals. They are just as gifted as anyone else, and often more gifted. But their inner opinion of themselves is small. They are continually surprised to find that they really can do well when they get into action. For them, life is largely a matter of learning to accept their own ability, to stop tearing themselves down . . . instead of thinking how they feel about something, to think rather of what is the first thing to DO about it. Then when they swing into action, their abilities come into play, and they surprise no one but themselves. (See illustration on page 110 for the physical proportion indicating the person inclined to underrate himself.)

If you have a narrow-faced child, the first day of school take that boy or girl completely into the classroom and put his hand in the kindergarten teacher's. (And don't look back if he starts crying.) The second day, leave him inside the classroom door. The third day, leave him down the hall. The fourth day, leave him inside the school entrance. The fifth day, let him out of the car at the curb. In a week after that, he'll be on his own completely, and even proudly bringing a chum home with him.

One of the marvelous things about life is that traits are subject to our conscious functioning direction. We can turn them on or off, just as we can turn our heads to one side or another. Better yet, we can even build certain traits, such as self-confidence. This is part of the game of life. It is a wonderful thing to see people grow from the inside out in the expression of their nature, like sprouting acorns.

Aristotle liked hawk-nosed generals. They suited him with their businesslike nature of getting the job done. His idea works out under statistical scrutiny, that men with Roman or hawk noses are rated by their acquaintances as being more commercial and administrative and businesslike. (Even the women you know who are built this way talk business or prices . . . they have a keen sense of values . . . they know that money does not

The roundish-faced (endomorphic) individual, especially with the roundish fore-head, is the home-lover, a natural hostess and an enjoyer of food preparation. In the long run, with a woman of this build, home will win out over career.

grow on trees—and their checks never bounce.) The person with the concave nose has the opposite gift, that of being ministrative or spontaneously helpful.

If you are choosing someone to handle money, select a man or woman with a convex nose. Other traits being equal, they not only will handle it more knowingly and with more facility—but will also enjoy it. Business and finance is a game with them. The money is used to keep score. They like to be paid for what they do. They like to pay for what they get, and not be under obligation.

If your husband has the commercial build, make him glow with happiness by telling him how you have saved some money in the way you have shopped. If your customer is built with with the commercial trend, he will go for bargains. If your employee is built commercially-minded, remind him of the cash bonuses available. (See illustration on page 114.)

Conversely, the individual with the retroussé or concave nose has something in his build indicating he is spontaneously helpful. He is happy being of service. He thinks in terms of human values. Money is just something to use to make people happy. If he is President, money is going to be spent freely and the national debt is going to go up.

If your wife is ministrative, with the scoopety, "ski-jump" nose (see illustration on page 116), she brightly assists you. If you are sick, she *shows* she is glad to nurse you out of it. (Whereas the Roman-nosed wife goes through the same motions but is serious-faced as if just carrying out her policy or her businesslike duty . . . she should learn to LOOK HAPPY to do it, so her inner intention gets across and she is not misunderstood as begrudgingly doing it.)

If you run a restaurant, choose the ministrative waitresses, and notice the personal way in which they serve their patrons. You do not feel like a bother to them when they wait on you. But if you are picking a payroll expert or an accountant, pick the Roman-nosed or hawk-nosed individual. For someone on a combination job, such as hostess-and-cashier, choose someone with an average nose, who can lean either direction.

And, oh yes! If you want to know where the bargains around town are, ask Mr. Roman Nose. He can tell you immediately . . . in fact, he has been wanting to get to some of them.

9. MEETING PEOPLE AND MAKING FRIENDS

There is something that passes between the eyes of people when they meet that tells more about how interested they are in each other, and how naturally drawn toward one another, than does a good deal of the ensuing conversation (or lack of it).

Salesmen know that the first 15 seconds is extremely important in meeting someone, in deciding how the interview or episode is going to go. Try to think of a single top salesman who doesn't flash his smile when introduced! He is his bright best self. He makes small talk and keeps the conversation going. He shows his interest in you, as a person, and in your needs.

Use your magnetism and your smiling optimism, and your good humor, in meeting people. Bring your best self to the surface. First impressions are important. Habits are important, too, so practice, at every opportunity, being your best self when meeting someone else (this includes practicing on your family at home—be as bright when they come into the room as you are when company comes in).

The broad-faced, broad-foreheaded individuals have self-confidence and can think in big terms. Everything else being equal, they are not easily impressed by others, and are thorough about what they do (and thorough about what they won't do.) This quality is part of this young woman's nature, along with other traits such as her generosity and good taste.

When meeting someone, as fast as possible use your face language, to have a "handle" to grab in approaching him as the individual he is. One of the first things to look at is the eyebrow placement. If the eyebrows are high above the eyes, at first say "Mr." or "Mrs." or "Miss" as the case may be—not Jim or Betty or Sharon. The selective person, with high brows, resents any apparent invasion of privacy or the taking of acquaintance-ship for granted. You wait for him (or her) to begin to treat you in a friendly way before you start to act like an old acquaint-ance.

With face language, instead of a trial and error waste of time and effort, you can approach immediately and definitely as the person is built, to click with him. (Just as YOU like to be approached in the way you are built to be approached.) What is one man's meat is another man's poison. What pleases one, irritates another.

Of course, the way is easier and all systems are "Go" if the other individual has an affable, amiable nature (indicated by eyebrows set down close to the eyes), and if he is broad-minded and easy-going, an enjoyer and has a sense of humor. (You remember the person with the broad view and easy-going na-ture is the one wide between the eyes . . . the enjoyer is the round-headed, round-faced endomorph . . . the individual with a well-developed sense of humor has the laugh lines radiating out from the outer corners of his eyes.)

Due to eye-contact, in meeting people, whether you remember their names is not nearly as important as the look in your eyes, which should be pleased, friendly and interested. You will find your eyes look more this way when you remember to use your face language, because it DOES make you look at

LOW EGO

them as a special individual (instead of some generality thrown in your way).

If someone is introducing you, the words you use are not nearly as important to the other person as the expression of pleasantness and interest on your face. A smile is the universal language. It helps get your spirit, the inner you, across. It is good procedure to smile when you have a photograph taken— you will look to others as a more likable person, one they would like to know.

If you know face language, your smile is not forced or

hypocritical. You know that across from you is someone who, like you, is good at heart, who has a special combination of traits through which he has to be reached . . . and who will respond and come to life when treated with interest as the individual he (or she) is. Your knowledge of that person's traits is an Open Sesame. Try it. You'll like the results. NOTE: Don't try this friendly, smiling, interested approach on people you don't really want to deal with—or you'll find it hard to get rid of them!

Before even deciding if you want to meet someone, you are

HIGH EGO

Looking at the most salient quality you recognize by face language often gives you a "handle" in how to approach an individual. This man has the aristocratic convex nose of the administrative and commercial inclination—you can anticipate that he will have a feel for money matters, prices and values. You can zero in on other qualities too, such as that his sparkling eye will mean he is an alert person with magnetism . . . and he has the rhetoric lines indicating that he loves the well-spoken and would be irritated by anything mispronounced.

inclined to size him up. In civilized life today, this is usually a casual matter with little at stake at the moment. In ancient times the situation might often be more crucial, such as when a force of invaders swept into your village and you had to decide on the instant which was the person to appeal to for justice. So usually you have plenty of time to gauge the other individual and decide if you want to strike up an acquaintance.

Would the other person be interesting or pleasant to know? Could the other person provide help or profit or companionship? Is it someone with whom a beautiful friendship might develop? You can see that what you have in mind will govern to a degree what you are looking for in the other person. If you are a stranger in New York and want to ask the way to Lexington Avenue, you would look around for someone with the concave nose denoting spontaneous helpfulness, who would be glad to assist you.

This scanning method of selecting a naturally helpful person was used successfully in Boston by a pineapple company sales executive who had studied face language. On a trip from California to the east coast, he was in a rented car. His automobile ran out of gas in heavy traffic in downtown Boston. Other drivers were honking at him to get out of the way. He waited a moment until he spotted a ministrative driver, waved to him and explained his problem. Mr. Ministrative pushed the visitor's car out of the thoroughfare with his own automobile, and saw that the Californian got his gasoline. And he did this *gladly!*

That's one of the things to anticipate about people in sizing them up. They are happy to do what is their natural inclination.

Conversely, they're irritated if you ask them to do something against their natural tendency.

If you are asking where you could obtain a bargain, you would ask the hawk-nosed person. He gets interested as he tells you about the best places to get a buy. If you want to find where the best food in town is, select a round-headed person with a moon-shaped face. He not only has a number of places in mind which he has explored with his gourmet trend. His face will light up, too, as he gets into his favorite subject. One of the advantages of using face language is that you can anticipate

COMMERCIAL

114

what the individual's reaction is going to be. This averts a lot of adverse reactions.

How do you size up the person who comes onto the plane and takes the seat next to you? The first thing to look for is whether that person has a high-brow build. If he or she has, you know you'd better take it easy about opening up a conversation, because that individual is going to take plenty of time before ever getting buddy-buddy.

If your seat-mate aboard plane has full, loose lips, he or she can prove quite voluminous in conversation. Noticing this, you may just occupy yourself with reading the airline magazine so you don't have to listen to too much talk on the trip, if it's your mood right now to be quiet or to have an opportunity to gather your thoughts.

The most important place to look is the other person's eyes. Generally speaking, avoid shifty-eyed individuals. They are not at peace with themselves, and are not going to be very dependable in carrying through anything they promise you. They may not try to sell you the Brooklyn Bridge, but their deceitfulness or lack of follow-through will amount to the same thing.

Somebody may give you just as much trouble who has a hard, brazen stare and a tough look. Some women may be this way, but usually it's the man who is tough and daring. The gloomy-eyed person has problems and needs to unload. The glassy-eyed individual is under pressure and may do the unpredictable.

On the plus side in people you size up, magnetism is a key desirable trait. It is indicated by sparkling eyes. You know this person is vital and lively, and can be a lot of fun.

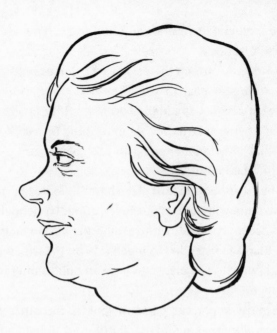

MINISTRATIVE

The laugh lines of humor mean you can expect the person to be more good-humored, everything else being equal . . . and, that you can kid that person once the amenities are over.

The person with the happy mouth is going to be more fun to be around. He or she is going to act much less like a sourpuss, as well as looking less droopy-mouthed.

The large-eyed individual is going to prove to be a warmer person, with more personality and with feelings more on the surface.

To a lesser degree, you can size people up from photographs in advance of meeting them. But this has its limitations, due to three dimensions being reduced to two. Also, you can best gauge traits from full head-on, or from full profile, and pictures so often are at a three-quarter slant of the face. But every cue you do get from the other person's structural indications helps you know that much more about how he is liable to function.

Remember, too, these traits work with children as well as with adults. If you see a broad-faced child, you know that child has a strong nature and can be talked to in a grown-up manner. If you see a narrow-faced child, you know that youngster has less inner self-confidence and should be dealt with only in terms of what is the easiest first thing to do.

Some approaches to understanding people are "after-the-fact" approaches, gauging their attitudes after they have already jelled (and often jelled to your disadvantage). Your success average will go up, and you will cry less often over spilled milk, if you first notice what their face language has to tell you.

There is a reason for the saying, "Birds of a feather flock together." You click more naturally with people of your own build. This build does not mean size or complexion, but rather the structural indicators you have learned earlier in this book, especially the indicators around the eyes and mouth.

If you have large, emotional eyes, you deal best with others of your kind, who are also warm and emotional. If you have full, generous lips, you get along best with others who are outgiving in their expression of words and generous with their time. If your eyes are wide apart, you feel most comfortable around others who are easy-going and broad in their views. If your eyebrows are straight and flat, you appreciate others who likewise are aesthetic and who want to make an art out of living.

Conversely, if you are small-eyed, tight-lipped, have eyes close together and "roof-top" shaped eyebrows, you get along best with others who likewise are matter-of-fact, concise, concerned and yet not dedicated to any form of art. But, by using your knowledge of face language, you can make friends wherever you go, much more easily than could before reading this book. The cues are right there in front of you, in the other person's visage.

If the person you meet has the concave nose and is ministrative, ask for his or her assistance. If he is the round-headed, moon-faced endomorph (the jolly, jovial enjoyer), ask where the best food in town is. If he is narrow-faced, remember he is on the self-conscious, modest side, and give him some compliments. If he has large eyes, talk about mutual acquaintances or his family. If he is tight-mouthed and has brief lips, be concise yourself and do not waste his time. If his eyebrows sit high above his eyes, remember your manners and call him "Mr." until you get to know him better. But if he has laugh-lines fanning out from the outer corners of his eyes, you can joke with him nevertheless. There is always a "handle" to take hold of to open the conversation, by noticing what trait indicator is pronounced and "jumps out" at you.

This knowledge is particularly valuable in traveling. You more quickly notice and understand others as individuals. You know better how to approach them, and how not to offend them.

Not only will these pointers help you make friends more

Even without face language, who could help but gain an impression that here's a cheerful person to be around? But actual knowledge is much more valuable than generalities. Now you can tell specifically that this woman has an unually good sense of humor . . . has plenty of magnetism and vitality . . . is dependable . . . craves harmony . . . has a gift with words.

quickly in new situations (such as I have found in traveling abroad), but it can also help you (at last!) make friends with relatives or associates with whom you never before could click. Try it. You will discover not only that you have a new and genuine interest in the other individual—and show this interest —but that you can more quickly tap his or her enthusiasms and get to talking. And you will appreciate that person more, knowing how to see his or her special gifts.

You will have a spin-off benefit, too, of expressing your own traits better. This is because you now know some of your own strong and weak points, from learning structure/function indications. Forewarned is forearmed. And, knowledge is power.

Will Rogers said, "We are all ignorant . . . we are just ignorant about different things." Conversely, we are all gifted —we are just all gifted in different ways.

Use your own talents liberally. If you have a sense of humor, use it freely. If you have the endomorph's roundish build, you are a born host. If you are affable, you can show people quickly that you have accepted them. If you have magnetism, you stand out in a group and are remembered . . . you attract others to you. If you have a strong broad-faced build, you can make others brighten up by telling them something you notice they do well, or giving them a compliment. If you are ministrative, ask how you can help.

Also, you can build some traits stronger than they are now, by exercise. If you are too timid and modest, welcome each proper opportunity to step up and introduce yourself. You will surprise no one more than yourself, and you will spread some happiness by making others feel noticed.

Should you have the turned-down (sourpuss) lips of the pessimist, you can build this up into the happy mouth of the optimist by practicing your big million-dollar smile on every mirror you come across, all day long—and by wearing a cheerful countenance at all times, and greeting every living creature with a smile. This must be genuine, too, so that your eyes as well as your lips are friendly . . . so that you are not just offering a mechanical grimace.

Should you wish to go further in your own self-understanding and self-improvement as an individual, based on your natural individuality, you can always feel free to contact the author (The Interstate College of Personology, 6600 Geary Boulevard, San Francisco, California 94121) for further information, the name of the nearest personologist to do your full analysis, or the nearest class for instruction by the Interstate College of Personology.

You have learned some of the key traits for dealing with others according to practical face language. But in all there are 68 traits statistically validated in personology, so there is a rich field in the World of Individuals if you wish to explore it more completely. Meanwhile you have plenty of ammunition to make a big change in your life when properly applied. Try it. You'll like the results, and so will all the new friends you make.

10. CONVERSATION

Talk to the other person's key trait—the one that "jumps out" at you when you look at him or her. This may be large eyes. It may be a round head. It may be a Roman nose.

If the person has large eyes, talk about the family, friends you both know, times you've had together . . . things on the sentimental side. Also offer a snack, or say, "Would you like a drink?" (Naturally the occasion, such as whether you are at a bar or in a church, will determine the details—but the general idea is the same, to talk about matters of sentiment, matters of the heart.)

Of course, if the person has small beady eyes, talk in a more matter-of-fact way and about more businesslike matters, and expect no effusiveness.

If the person to whom you are talking has the round, jovial build of the conserving endomorph, food is a choice subject. Comment, "My, that was a nice appetizer!" Ask what made it so tasty. Or talk about the home or apartment—the endomorph's life is centered around where he or she lives.

If your conversation partner is the square-headed mesomorph, talk about career and projects. Should you be talking to a Roman-nosed individual (convex nose) talk business and prices. Ask, "How did the stock market do today?" Or, "How much did that cost?"

If your conversation partner has the concave, "ski-jump" nose of the helpful person, ask for some assistance. I know of one woman who got rides to work from a man merely by mentioning to him that she was having trouble with the battery in her car. The rides to work led to a romance. Another example—policemen and state patrolmen, and others in the protective services, usually have the same helpful build . . . notice how one of them brightens up when you ask how to get to such and such a location. People *enjoy* doing what they're built to do.

The thin-faced, more self-conscious person glows when you give him or her a compliment. The dictionary says a compliment is *merited* praise—so let it be a true compliment, such as about promptness or a beautiful smile (so it is not soft-soaping and doesn't sound like soft-soaping).

If you are conversing with a broad-faced, self-confident man, woman or child, you are facing a strong genetic build, but it is still a good technique to talk more "You" and less "I." Franklin D. Roosevelt had this gift. He had a visitor from California. He asked the Californian, "Where are you from?" —and as soon as he knew which city, mentioned mutual acquaintances. Then he asked about the visitor's occupation and interests. When the interview was over, all of a sudden the California publisher realized that the President had learned a lot from him, but that he hadn't learned anything from the President (except how to be a good conversationalist, which after all, is quite a bit).

If you are talking to a soft person, don't be bothered by their whining . . . such people whine to everybody. Be pronouncedly cheerful, to keep up your own vibration as well as to help the others.

Conversing with a hard person, such as a coal miner or a lumber-jack (or some chorus girls!) don't be bothered by their apparent toughness and lack of response initially. They just SEEM unresponsive, because of their hard shell. When they do respond from the core, they respond fully.

With the thick-skinned, coarse-grained individual, use a louder tone of voice—much as if they were twice as far off. They like heartiness and vigor. No gentle hints.

With the thin-skinned, baby-haired person, turn on your genteel nature and your finesse and subtlety. Keep your voice down. Keep the subject matter on the refined side, at least initially.

The analytical person has to be told "why," or you'll lose him or her in the conversation at some turn where you made a statement but didn't tell the reason. Don't just say, "I'm sorry I'm late," but first explain WHY you became late. The individual without analyticalness is bothered if you spend time telling "why." The thin-lipped, concise person wants you to get to the point. And let the mouthy, full-lipped person talk. You won't need to.

Be careful of what you say around perfectionists whose eyes are close together—make no sweeping statements. And do not talk politics or religion unless yours happens to be the same as theirs. Talk to them about their accomplishments and opinions. They always have a suggestion on something that could be done better.

There is a good side conversationally to every trait. The critical person (with the sharp-shooter's eye slanting down

With face language, you can go beyond the usual exclamation of "What a lovely picture of mother and daughter!" You can begin to notice what kind of people they are, as real persons. You notice that the mother has a fine sense of humor, is optimistic, helpful, fair-minded, generous, adventurous, and has a feel for the dramatic. But after all, you cannot see too much from this view of the young girl except that she is sensitive, helpful, and likes surprises. But from the profile picture you realize that also she is a trusting and artistic youngster, and rather concise for a child.

from the nose to the outside) loves to give advice. And it is good advice. (And it's free!) I recall the first time I was editing a newspaper, and I had an undertaker friend who was highly critical. All I had to do was ask him what *he* would do about a particular civic situation, and he always came out with something good. I had no more need to do much talking after pressing his "hot button" of conversation.

With face language, you can keep the initiative in conversation. As the saying goes in sports, the best defense is a good offense. While your conversation partner is responding verbally to a question you gave him or her because you noticed the first outstanding trait, you have time to keep looking in an admiring and interested way, and spot other key traits to which to talk. Don't stare while doing this. Staring is not natural, and makes the other individual feel uneasy. Just be casual and follow the eyes. You will pick up the other traits peripherally.

You will find soon that you can open up people conversationally . . . even relatives with whom you never used to click. You understand them, even if they do not understand you as a person. Their liking for you sky-rockets. After all, you are paying alert and interested and favorable attention to them, as individuals. Everyone likes to be noticed and appreciated as a person in their own right. Your face language helps you get through the "membrane" between the two of you. And after that, you always converse easily, as old friends . . . which you now are!

The choosy, selective individual with high brows turns out to be a wonderful, all-out person, properly approached . . . whereas previously you had regarded that person as opinionated, stuck-up, distant. That individual is usually quite lonely because of the wrapping of reserve he or she is built to carry around . . . and is very relieved and pleased to have someone else take the lead in the conversation.

Of course, with the choosy individual you must take it easy at first in the conversation, and go through channels. First talk about "community" topics which anyone can observe, such as, "My, the weather turned out beautifully today!" or "What a beautiful picture there on the wall!" At first talk about nothing personal about yourself or the other individual. And, talk in the same casual tone of voice as you do about the weather, so you do not seem pushy or cross-examining like a district attorney (this is especially important if you have a big ego).

Use the "W" questions (words that start with "w") as the "shepherd's crooks" which pull the other person close to you. Usually these are the journalisitic "what," "where," "why," "when" and "who" (the "five little men who taught Kipling all he knew.") You do not need to talk about yourself. Just talk about the other person. And talk only about what makes him or her look good, such as "What a smooth driver you are! Where did you learn to drive?" (And never, "Where did you get that black eye?") You merge into the complimentary, more personal questions AFTER talking about impersonal things, with the high-browed, discriminative human being.

One woman who had me do her personology analysis had been a USO hostess during World War II. She said you would be surprised at how many GIs were bashful. Some "W" questions she used, which she found got them talking comfortably and animatedly with little effort on her part, were: "What kind of a bird would you like to be if you were a bird?" and "If you were an animal, what kind of an animal would you prefer to be?" (Aristotle would have been pleased to know that they always answered the kind they most looked like!)

Besides helping others enjoy conversation with you, you help them unfold. They have been waiting a long time to find someone interested in them who is not just interested in himself. You will easily find many delightful acquaintances. And you will learn much interesting information from them. (Just ask the person with laugh-lines what was the funniest thing that ever happened to him in his travels, and the two of you will have a wonderful time chuckling about it!)

You already know all you know. But if you ask successful men the secret of their success . . . trim people the secret of keeping their weight down . . . a golfer what has been his best score, and what has helped him most to improve his game . . . you learn some valuable tips your self. And you are into the wonderful World of Individuals!

11. MAKING YOUR FACE LOOK APPEALING

Have you ever thought that there is NO one in the world just like *you* . . . just as no one else has your fingerprints?

Be personological. Play up your individuality. Move the decimal point over. Imitate no one. Be your best self. Blossom.

If you are a man with robust, rugged texture (with good thick skin and coarse hair) keep a tan and have a hearty appearance.

If you as a woman have a dainty build, accentuate it. Keep the makeup in good taste. Avoid the garish. Avoid anything that seems false. Be YOU. It will come off better. You can't really imitate anyone else well anyway.

If you have an aristocratic, Roman nose (like Barbra Streisand or Frank Sinatra) act aristocratic. You will attract others who have the same build, and who like your kind. If you have the ministrative concave nose (like Julie Andrews or Glenn Ford) be your natural helpful self, focusing more on the other person's needs.

If you had one percent of the money spent today in the

129

United States by people trying to make their faces look better visually, you would be rich. You could live off the interest. Yet more than a third of American marriages end in divorce. The veneer is not nearly as important as the natural self.

Be your own kind, and play that up. Others who are built like you will be attracted to you. Birds of a feather flock together . . . and they get along better together.

It's like the song goes,

> "Be what yo' is,
> 'Cause if yo' is what yo' ain't,
> Yo' ain't what yo' is!"

If you have full, rich lips, accentuate them. If you have fine teeth, use your flashy smile. If you have a perky build, use perky styling and act pert. If you have large eyes, let go and express your feelings warmly in happy situations. If you are a woman and are the bashful type, play up the helpless ingenue role. Act admiring. Ask for advice or help.

Right now, you are finding yourself taking inventory of yourself, possibly for the first time in your life. Take a piece of paper and make a list of just how YOU are the unique individual you are. Make a list of your personological traits which stand out, from those you have learned in this book. Are you dramatic or aesthetic? Are you the enjoyer or the builder? Are you the indoor or outdoor variety?

From your list, play up the qualities that draw others to you, such as magnetism, emotionality, generosity, optimism, humor, helpfulness, broad-mindedness, and jolly joviality.

Put your best foot forward. Play down fussy qualities you

may have built up, such as methodicalness, details concern or exactingness.

Get rid of unfavorable temporary indicators, such as glassy eyes from missing sleep or being on the run instead of having your routine in hand. Shed your worry lines by doing things carefully in the first place and then dismissing them from your mind . . . no post-mortems . . . keep your youthfulness of approach and visage.

Do what Benjamin Franklin did when he was getting ahead in life. He worked systematically on a trait a week. (He figured out 13 factors on which he thought he could improve, and took one a week, repeating the cycle every quarter.) In his autobiography, he mentions that detail-concern (indicated personologically by the knotted, cloudy brow) was the hardest trait to get rid of.

Ask yourself what made you attracted to the people who are now your closest friends or dear ones. Possibly you NO-TICED them at first because they stood out in some unique or attractive way. But what in the long run has drawn you to them is that they FACIALLY always showed an interest and liking for you, every time you came around. You may not have inherited a classic profile, but probably no one of your friends has one either. You can attract people by having a pleasant, interested visage . . . and consistently just being you, but your very best self. It will attract more people to you than getting your face lifted (and be less expensive).

If you are going to be visually bright-eyed and appealing, there are some prices to pay in taking care of your physical mechanism . . . getting to sleep before midnight, for example. But if you follow the Benjamin Franklin program of working

131

Here is an unfolding personality—affectionate, lively and dramatic, but discriminating . . . and, magnetic, alert, generous and sympathetic.

Here is an unusual face, a face you would study . . . a face of contrasts . . . a very *individual* individual! Face language gives you some cues to this interesting nature. The firmness is apparent . . . it may be slow coming, but when it comes, it will be all-out. There is no flabbiness. But the lips give a cue of a generous, outpouring nature . . . once the analytical nature (indicated by the eyes) is satisfied. And the esthetic nature must have, in the long run, harmony and beauty.

133

on a trait a week to improve yourself, you will find yourself enjoying many spin-off benefits.

You have an inner right to put yourself forward, if your motive is fair and you are just being your own true self. If you polka, dance it with your own special flourish. Let go and be you! You can be your own self more fully when some day you have your full structure/function analysis performed by a personologist—when you know how you stand on all 68 traits instead of only the introductory ones. But you know enough now to give you the idea, and put you on the track . . . and also to notice other people interestedly and cue yourself in to their orbit.

Every woman can be graceful, in her own way. Every man can be interesting, in his own way.

From now on, try this: consistently being your own self and your best self—and being interested in the other person in his own right and helping him unfold to his full potential. Look in the mirror when you are doing this, and you will see that you are animated and appealing. And it will click, because it is natural. And it will last, because it is from the inside, not from the outside.

Your hair style should harmonize with your natural build —and accentuate it. If you are a man with a rugged fiber and a bushy build, a swashbuckling moustache may suit your style. If you are a man with silkier hair and more finely-chiseled features, a smaller moustache and more finely-defined beard may be more "You."

Generally speaking, beard and moustache make a man seem more masculine and formidable . . . and the clean-shaven man appears less threatening. But this is an individual matter. A man with the broad face of the self-confident, plus strong jaw and chin, may appear plenty strong and formidable in his own clean-shaven appearance. Abraham Lincoln had such a strong face that, unshaven, he looked sad or unfriendly—a girl who admired him wrote she thought he would get more votes with a beard, so he grew one . . . in a way, a mild beard shielded his more formidable-appearing strong face.

It has been said that women are attracted to interesting-looking men, who might be pretty special to know for some reason—and that men are attracted to women who are pretty. While this is an oversimplification, there is something to it. What makes general statements difficult to use is that individuals vary in their tastes and preferences. One man is built so slim girls are appealing to him. Another man is attracted by the more buxom "meat and potatoes" variety. And there are so many people, somewhere you can find one to suit your choice. For every Jack, there is a Jill.

You are wise if you try simply to be the best of your own kind. If you are the career kind, be the best you can at it. If you are a born homemaker, enjoy being the best homemaker possible.

Likewise with makeup. Nature builds in harmony. A woman is wise if, as a natural blonde, she never dyes her hair black . . . it wouldn't be natural, and it wouldn't go with her complexion or eyebrows.

Have you heard of genic syndromes? Eye color, skin color

and hair color usually harmonize. Very few blonds have olive skin. Titian hair is more liable to go with a peaches and cream complexion.

The eyebrows fit in. So if you are going to tint your hair, you should tint your eyebrows, too, or they will be out of harmony.

Because of genetic syndromes, you are most effective in dyeing your hair if you simply tint it more along its natural direction—such as perhaps making Titian hair more red-headed. Move the decimal point over more toward your natural direction, not in the opposite direction.

If you have been graying and want to look more youthful, the tinting or dyeing should be more of a return to your former, more youthful color, than to some other variety of color not yours by nature.

Genetic syndromes work in many areas. People with large feet usually have large hands. People with long fingers usually have long toes. The same is true of facial features. There is a rhythm, a symmetry, a unity to the kind of features a person has. Bob Hope's nose would not look right on Frank Sinatra, and vice versa. Because of the genic syndromes in the face, your nose goes naturally with your own individual kind of face. A different nose would look odd on you.

A San Francisco businesswoman had her nose altered—but then she wanted her old nose back! She originally had an aristocratic, convex, Roman nose, a bit on the hawk side. She thought it made her look too self-sufficient. She had it altered by plastic surgery. The new nose was retroussé, concave—it made her look ministrative, more on the helpless side. But she still had naturally the same businesslike nature as before the plastic surgery.

She had always been the shrewd, alert, sharp, businesslike person. And she still was—and she still talked that way. Nothing had been altered except the facial indicator. She held her own with the men in conversation. She had much of interest to contribute.

Formerly, the men used to cluster around her at a cocktail party, to hear her wisecracks and witticisms. But now they left her alone. That administrative talk didn't seem right coming from such a helpless-looking, naive-appearing female. She wanted her old nose back, so the men would cluster around her again.

Because of the genic syndromes, a person's grooming will usually click best if the eyebrows are not altered too much. They should be permitted to follow their natural line, or to have that line accentuated—such as the dramatic, arched eyebrow given even more flair . . . or the inverted chevron eyebrow made even more striking.

If one eyebrow is by nature quite different from the other, it should not be worked over to try to make it appear the same . . . any more than you would try to get the fingerprints on one hand to try to match the prints on the other hand. Due to getting a set of 23 chromosomes from each parent, everyone has a somewhat different build on one side than the other (and a different profile.) So if a person was made into complete symmetry, he would look odd and not natural.

Eye shadow applied more toward the outer part of the eyes will make a woman's eyes look further apart and give her a more open-minded, tolerant appearance, if her eyes are by nature very close set. A thin-lipped woman will look more outgoing and generous in her appearance if she spreads her lipstick beyond the borders of her lips. But the mouth can quickly be made cheerful and appealing by using a smile and a cheerful appearance—and that will bring a more permanent benefit by also helping an optimistic quality become more second-nature.

Practice more with your mirror. Make sure the corners of your mouth are used to being pulled up. Say good-bye to the sourpuss! As you know, it takes fewer muscles to smile than to frown.

Shedding the worry lines between your eyebrows will also make you look more attractive. Do this by being less fussy . . . less of the perfectionist . . . less of the doublechecker—be careful in the first place and do things well, but then dismiss them from your mind—no post-mortems—no worrying.

For magnetic eyes, LISTEN WITH YOUR EYES as well as your ears, when you are talking to someone important to you. Bright, interested, friendly eyes, and a cheerful mouth, can do a great deal to make your face look appealing and attractive. If you will notice people you know who attract others, you will see this is true. So use these gifts yourself. They are instantly available and they cost nothing—but they can bring you rich rewards, both in being more popular with others, and in unfolding your own nature to its full potential.

12. DATING, MARRIAGE AND SEX

I have a hobby of asking couples how they found each other. Always it's some very natural way. Neither dropped out of the sky with a parachute. Usually it's through mutual acquaintances. A friend says, "I know just the girl (or just the fellow) you ought to meet." Many men have married a sister of a friend. Many women have married a brother of a friend. A lot of people met the person of their destiny while filling in for someone else. Some people have ended up becoming attached to their friend's partner on a double date.

On occasion I have seen a bashful girl encouraged to accept a date from a man she didn't particularly like, because of the opportunity of meeting other men as she went places, and in that way running across the man of her dreams.

I have never met anyone who knew, the fateful morning before meeting the individual who was that person's destiny, that it was any different from any other morning, or was going to be the "day of days!"

One young woman cried her heart out because no one dated her, let alone proposed marriage. Mrs. Whiteside suggested that she look around first among the men where she worked . . . in other words, start with "what's in the cupboard," before seeing if she needed to look further.

This young woman worked on a daily newspaper. She noticed an unattached young assistant editor who was a very quiet individual and always seemed wrapped up in his work. From then on, she "just happened" to be around him quite a bit, and to be very pleasant and complimentary. One thing led to another. They began dating, and married. Now they have an ideal family. The young mother is just back from taking the children on a trip to Europe. So, gold is where you find it.

Men have traits, just as women have traits. It is a surprise to some girls to find out that there are bashful men, who need to be coaxed as far as making dates. (From then on, they may prove as physically voracious as their brothers, but that is another side of their nature.)

Usually it is the thin-faced man of less self-confidence who needs more coaxing, and to be led forward a step at a time. The broad-faced man has more sense of his own power and ordinarily takes over more quickly, and is more rapidly audacious.

Thin-faced women too, of course, are less self-confident and less sure of themselves, and need to be led forward a step at a time. (Personological research has shown that, except for the sex-linked characteristics, women have the same traits as men and, according to their individual proportions, can likewise be as stubborn or mercenary or courageous or adventurous —or modest and bashful, as the case may be.) Each person is a human being, with the same traits but in different proportions. So each person is a new equation. This is where your face language comes in handy.

Look at the girl on the cover of this book. If you are an

unattached man, you would like a date with her. Why? Your face language tells you that she would be charming, affectionate, optimistic, fair-minded, dramatic, lively, with a large vocabulary, and is an enjoyer. She has beauty. But she has more. She is a magnetic and agreeable person.

If you are an unattached woman reading this volume, which of the men photographed in this book would you want to date? Which seems to you the most interesting or desirable personality? You have enough cues from traits you have learned in this book already, to anticipate what the man you are drawn toward would turn out like in personal acquaintance. You look beyond the transitory hairstyling. You look beyond factors such as complexion which are decorative but have no known personological significance.

What do you have in mind in dating? It is a world of individuals, so different people have different objectives. If what you have in mind is only a pleasant episode of dining out, going to the theatre, or skiing, with nothing more intimate or permanent involved, then you are only out for fun with an agreeable companion—there is less at stake, and you do not have to be as selective.

If you are an aggressive man or woman, then you have more in mind than food and entertainment. You are heading toward a more high-voltage situation. But in the back of your mind you are still like the early Spanish explorer looking for gold, hoping to find the long-sought treasure . . . in your case, the treasure is someone with both the physical and personal attributes to build a beautiful relationship that left nothing to be desired—which could lead to something perfect and permanent, and end your searching.

Momentary expressions can be of value. The laugh lines at the outer corners of the eyes show here's a person with a sense of humor, with whom you can kid and joke. Upturned lips are the cue to an optimistic bent. The bright eyes show magnetism and an interest in life.

142

If your goal, clear-cut in the front of your mind, or hidden in the back of your mind, is to find a permanent partner, then you should look for someone who matches your personality. Then you will click together. You will have less adjusting to do. You will see more eye to eye, if your eyes are spaced the same —if you are the close-eyed perfectionist, gravitate toward a mate likewise close between the eyes. If you are broad between the eyes, you will get along better with someone else who takes a broad view, and seldom manifests indignation.

If you are large eyed and emotional, select another sentimentalist. If you are matter-of-fact, pick out someone who, like you, has small irises.

If you are the robust, hearty outdoor person who doesn't need hot and cold running water, pick someone who also has a rugged, thick-skinned nature and fibre.

It is valuable to have some cues to the other person's basic abiding disposition, so you know what they are going to be like in the long run. It is indeed true that very few people—men or women—run after they have caught the bus. We naturally put our best foot forward to make a good impression (some people more than others, of course, due to personological differences).

The momentary expressions on the face give you an idea of how things are going. But how things are going at the moment pretty much reflects whether you have paid attention to how the other person is built as an individual and acted accordingly. The other person's expression of the moment shows whether you have pressed the hot button, so to speak . . . or, have "blown it" by neglecting the obvious trait to which you should have directed your words and actions.

Remember to do the Benjamin Franklin technique of working systematically on a trait of yours every week, to get your habit patterns down to second-nature and express your own traits well. This is so that you will be your best self and more likely to appear attractive to the individual you have been looking for, and who has been looking for you.

While I was writing this section of the book, a ship's captain came in and said to expect a call from a young couple, friends of his on shore. He explained that the young man and woman, college students, had an LTA (living-together-arrangement), but now had started to quarrel and were not getting along. Also, the girl wanted to get married. She wanted social approval. The young man's parents looked down on her because of what she was doing. Now, the quarrels must end so that a marriage could begin and last.

There is a law of nature that nothing stands still, particularly with a man and a woman. The tendency is either for them to get more cozy or to drift further apart.

Perhaps you've seen a movie illustrating this fact. Robert Mitchum and Deborah Kerr starred in such a film. It had to do with World War II in the Pacific. Mitchum played the part of a hard-boiled Marine. Miss Kerr played the devoted nun. By happenstance of war, they were shipwrecked on the same island. They were the only Americans on the island, which was overrun by Japanese. While hiding out, the Marine blew up some vital Japanese supplies, the nun cooperating, and while they were celebrating, he ran across some saki. Although he was "married" to the Corps, and she was devout in her vows, their relationship threatened to get cozy indeed—until, of course, the American rescuers arrived in time and retook the

Here is an example of a mature woman whose face is appealing and beautiful, free of worry lines (just as her eyes are full of charm and her mouth is cheerful and pleasant). The horizontal lines keep the youthfulness of expression—they are the laugh lines at the outer edges of the eyes (and also the rhetoric lines which fan out from the nose horizontally beneath the eyes).

island . . . and the bachelor Marine and the nun went their separate ways.

There is no such thing as a lasting neutral relationship between two human beings thrown together by themselves for a long period of time. They must take some kind of a status—friends, enemies, an armed truce, or whatever their builds dictate as modified by the situation.

In a way, it could be called "the law of multiplication." If you are involved with someone else romantically and wish to build a lasting relationship, you will find that approaching your partner according to your partner's traits is an insurance policy for progress in the relationship. Really, now, how else can you approach another person except through their individual nature? How can anyone click with you except through your traits? As Aristotle put it, indeed, we are never faced with the universal, but always with the particular.

General resolutions are fine, but specific actions are what bring them into reality and permanence. If you want to please someone who has the aristocratic, commercially-minded build, give that person plenty of spending money. If you want to grow closer to someone who has the ministrative, helpful disposition, ask that person for help, in some way that is real and natural. If they collect books, ask to borrow a rare volume—then send a sincere thank you note when you return it. If the other person is analytical, ask him or her to help you figure something out. You grow closer to someone by doing things together.

It's not the *quantity* of time two people spend together that counts, but the *quality*. Romeo and Juliet had only three days together, and the world is still talking about it.

Your face language gives you "handles" to take hold of,

to grow closer to the other person. If your partner is round-headed—the jolly, jovial enjoyer, the endomorph strong on food and beverage, and gregarious—entertain that person, or take that person out to dine. If your partner is square-headed —the career man or woman, the mesomorph—draw him or her out with *friendly* leading questions. (And NO questions which make the person look bad, such as "Whatever happened to that traffic ticket you got?")

Everybody needs a cheerleader. They know their own faults. No one needs anyone to tell them about those. But a pal is somebody who is on your side regardless, who likes you just as you are—and who even enjoys your foibles and perhaps joins you in them!

When my son knew I would be writing this book, he said: "Be sure to include the trait of *criticalness.*" Statistics show that criticalness breaks up more relationships than any other trait. So if your eyes are slanting down at the outside (the sharp-shooter's eyes)—save your criticalness for work, where it can get you promoted as the expert or specialist. But off the job, use it ONLY for COMPLIMENTS. Think and talk only about the *redeeming quality* of the person or situation. And—do not worry about making anyone else perfect until *you* are perfect . . . work on your own traits, and accept the other person as he or she is. There will be plenty of time—after you get yourself in hand—to coach others to follow your example. (Actually, you will be much more charitable about others if you are working diligently on a trait a week yourself.)

Your eagle-eye of criticalness has an advantage when you use it for compliments—your compliments are specific and true, and long-remembered. There is a law of layers, too, in

Why are you reading this book? Because you always have noticed how much faces and expressions tell you, without a word being spoken. This picture is a striking example. Besides the friendly and alert expression which anyone could notice, from face language you know that here is a young wman of high courage and ability to express herself, and a feel for the dramatic and theatrical . . . that she is thorough but selective . . . and generous and broad-minded.

building a lasting relationship. The layers can be speeded, but they cannot be skipped. You have to be a friend before you can be a sweetheart. Your dear one has to know you *like* him or her, as well as *love* him or her.

If rather than being an affable, amiable individual, you are by nature more on the reserved and discriminative side, work at being less high-browed in approaching others. Show more that you *have* accepted them. Every time you enter the room where they are . . . or they enter the room where you are . . . or you recognize their voice on the phone—treat them like long-lost friends you had been hoping to hear from!

Talk to the other person's key trait, and you will be forced to improve yourself to do so, by tuning up your use of your own traits to their higher potential.

If someone is drifting away from you whom you want to keep—or if you wish to have an even richer and more solid relationship with someone permanently attached to you—make a list of that person's key traits according to the face language factors sequentially illustrated in this book. Then every week do three things that person would like according to his or her traits. And avoid doing three things you know would annoy.

Implement your desires with specific actions tailored to that one individual, and you never need worry about the fruitful outcome. It will come automatically, just as you would respond if someone treated you that way.

The woman of strong personality (broad-faced) should pat her man's face, wink at him, stroke his hair, scrub his back, and tickle his toes . . . even coo a bit. Then he is as happy as a clam at high tide. She never needs to worry about getting into a mother role.

She should never advise, remind, suggest or correct, unless asked (no matter how helpful she feels). This is particularly important if her man is narrow-faced and lacks self-confidence, and is always taking defensively whatever she says.

The strong-natured woman should, of course, run her own departments. But when off her "own 10 acres," she should make her man feel needed in the way a man is needed. If he volunteers to help her carry a heavy package, she should not slap his wrists mentally by saying, "No, I can manage."

When leaving her 10 acres and going out on the mutual "3 acre" territory between her domain and his, she should always wear something to remind him that she is entering the masculine-and-feminine area, and to be a success there of her gender. Entering the togetherness-territory, she should wear a beauty mark, eye shadow, high heels, pin on a lace handkerchief, or put a ribbon or a flower in her hair. If she is in doubt as to what to do, the rule-of-thumb indeed is: do what any other woman would do, if that woman were trying to get her meat hooks into her man.

The woman always knows what she *should* do to hold her man, or to make herself desirable to him in the first place. She is just fighting her own traits. If she gets herself in hand, ordinarily she can click beautifully with him.

The same goes for the man. If he and his woman have much in common, and he will just talk to her traits and work on his own, usually they can get along just fine. Since men have less at stake, so seldom getting pregnant, they can appear less predatory in the short range. But in the long range, the equation must balance, for nature indeed abhors a vacuum.

Doug Pledger, the radio commentator, put it well: "A wife can never be sure she is the only woman her husband has loved, but she can be sure that she is the only one who could make him prove it!"

In winning the best mate, you are starting a life-long program where you must bear in mind your mate's native preferences and disposition. Here your face language helps you be specific and effective. You are seldom faced with a whole personality at a time. Usually it's the key trait most connected with the momentary situation with which you must deal.

You have much knowledge now with which to get yourself across well. In this book you have already learned the indicators for:

Exactingness
Conciseness
Emotionality
Magnetism
Gloominess
Criticalness
Generosity
Optimism
Pessimism
Dramatic
Aesthetic
Discriminativeness
Affableness
Analyticalness
Humor
Oral Self-Expression

Rhetoric
Detail Concern
Methodicalness
Texture
Hardness or Softness
Conservation
Construction
Tolerance
Ego (Self-Confidence)
Commercial-Mindedness
Ministrativeness
(Plus, of course, expressions
    indicating current feelings.)

Quite a list, isn't it?

For anyone important in your life, take a 3×5 card and check the above list. Jot down on the card the traits which are outstanding about that person. Then refer back to the chapters telling what to do to deal with a person effectively who has those particular traits.

Don't tell the individual you are working on his or her traits to get yourself across better, but SHOW that person in a noticeable way how you are harmonizing with his or her build. Your dividends will come fast (just as *you* would respond well to anyone who liked and respected you as an individual, and tried to fit in with what is important to you).

You will find that this works excellently not only in winning the mate you desire, but in holding that mate. The individual's genetic coding is not going to change much during life. And your best way to fit in agreeably and be appreciated is not to try to change your mate or make your mate over, but to like your mate as he or she is, and to SHOW that you do!

Much of your trial-and-error in lovemaking has been due to trying to approach the other individual in a vague way, as a generality. You will have much more success as you approach the other person specifically, as the particular individual that person is.

Approach your love partner FIRST AS AN INDIVIDUAL, and secondly as a member of the opposite sex. You will find this works much better. And you will find also that your face language knowledge gives you keys to use.

The woman with an affectionate nature needs to be loved and caressed, and to have sweet things whispered to her, before action moves into the intimate stage. She needs to be loved primarily for her own sake, and to know how much you care for her as the special individual she is in her own right. Then she can let go and respond with her full warmth. (It is good strategy occasionally—when she can stand the shock!—just to hold her in your arms for a long time and lovingly say dear things to her, without demanding sex, simply to show her how much you love her as a person rather than as a convenience.)

On the other hand, the small-eyed woman, with buried emotions, can be more matter-of-fact and proceed into intimacy with less sentimental preparation.

The fine-textured woman, with the fine skin and baby hair, is inwardly revolted at anything coarse. She can be very sensitive and responsive once involved, but initially while she is getting into the spirit of things, should be treated with refine-

Yes, this is the same young woman! From the front-face view you see she has the roundish, oval face of the born homemaker, with a knack for everything that goes to making an enjoyable home . . . that she has a jolly side, would be good with food and entertaining. You notice too that she has a rather just sense of what should or should not be tolerated—that she would be conscientious enough to get things done, but narrow enough in her views to be unduly complaining.

But the profile also tells you that she has an aristocratic, Roman-nosed side to her nature . . . wants to take her time to figure things out, and not be rushed . . . and can be sharp in her observations.

ment. The woman of more robust build, with coarser features and more natural fibre to her hair, can stand grosser approaches.

The choosy, more discriminative woman (whose eyebrows are high above her eyes) cannot respond completely if she lacks privacy and knows someone may be listening. Her opposite, the earthy, affable woman, can fit in more easily to approaches which to many would not seem in good taste.

Everything else being equal, the narrow-faced, self-conscious woman is more timid, and less liable to be audacious about entering thoroughly into situations. She needs to be led a step at a time. She needs praise and assurance. She welcomes a strong shoulder on which to lean.

Here are some other axioms of face language which should prove especially helpful: The woman with a small mouth is more brief and concise, whereas the woman with large lips is more generous and giving. The tight-mouthed woman is more deliberate, but the woman with a protruding mouth is more impetuous and quicker to decide. The woman with laugh lines at the outer edges of the eyes enters situations more good-humoredly, and can be kidded more safely in courting and foreplay.

The woman wide between the eyes is broad-minded and easy-going, and hates to be mean. But, the woman whose eyes are close together is hard to please—she can be quite uncooperative if her man has done something previously that she doesn't like . . . and she wants to have everything perfect in the surroundings and procedure. Her man should tread lightly, and be careful about anything he might say or do which might offend.

When traits like these are paid attention to, and your loved one is approached the way she is built to be approached (which is also the way she *likes* to be approached), then as her man watches her eyes and expression and heightening of skin color, he is more likely to see those gauges giving favorable ratings.

Men have traits, too. The large-eyed man appreciates his dear one's eyes glowing fondly . . . her caresses . . . her rapturous or even passionate kisses. He appreciates the warmth of her personality ahead of intimate episodes. She's "mushy." So is he. They click great.

The matter-of-fact man with small beady eyes has to watch out or he will approach his dear one as a piece of meat on the table.

The man with little self-confidence usually has a narrow face in the forehead area. He appreciates some welcoming and build-up from his partner. He can even fail to function and appear impotent if she criticizes him or talks negatively.

The methodical man, with the knobby brow, too often fails to be creative. He follows a routine pattern. His beloved even knows what he is going to do (and when he is going to do it) before *he* does. He's quite liable to save his intimate episodes for Saturday night since he can sleep late Sunday. He should be more imaginative and show he is not in a rut. If his woman can stand the shock, he should fill the room with balloons sometime!

The aristocratic, commercially-minded man (with the convex nose) appears businesslike round the clock. He must be careful to show outwardly his inward joy and willingness, so that his partner doesn't think he is grudging what he is giving and that he is just carrying out his duty. He should LOOK HAPPY to do what he is if he is doing, if he is willing, so his mate doesn't say, "Well, to_____with you if you don't want to." (All the other person has to gauge by are the expressions of the face, the words used, and how much alacrity is demonstrated.)

The concave-nosed man has no such problems. He has a button of spontaneous helpfulness that can be pressed. He is glad to be needed, and to serve, and to be of help, especially if the needs are explained. (His problems are in the other areas of life, such as learning how to handle money.)

There are two things that every human being requires: to be loved, and to feel worthwhile. A thorough knowledge of face language enables you to better express these feelings.

Remember: Behind the surface traits that can be directed there is a whole person, a total self, a human being . . . needing to be loved and to feel some dignity.

This is just as true with a man as with a woman. (You know this if you are a man—you are more mechanical in build than a female, but after the novelty and convenience of having your woman available rubs off, you want to be liked and loved and respected as a human being, an individual in your own right, just as everyone else does.)

You can read (and probably have) books on the mechanics of lovemaking, as far as nerve endings and positions go. But the bliss which even the poets find difficulty in describing, of two people who care for each other, showing how glad they are to blend fully together in body, mind and spirit—this bliss and the resultant afterglow will be achieved more often as you use your face language to more completely reach the rich inner self of your partner as that partner is built uniquely to be reached.

Being naturally photogentic helps, but you can see how much more appealing a person you appear to be if you keep your mouth happy and your eyes lively.

Marriage has sex on its side—yet a lot of marriages break up. This because there are more traits to a person than sex drive, and these other traits can get in the way. Once a person gets involved in doing something, he or she can often let go and go all out. But making that first decision is where other traits come in.

Let me give an illustration about getting into the spirit of something once it's under way (an illustration from a different field of activity). Two teen-age brothers were having fun, and splattered mud on the walls of the family carport. Their father, a strict man, brought them paint and brushes—he made them do a repainting job. And once they got engaged in the painting project, they really enjoyed it.

It is the same with making love. Sex is as natural and right as the rain. But two people who love each other may feud and fight about OTHER things and have very little sex in their life, or what they do have may be of very poor quality. They may use sex like a fly-swatter, shutting off the other person's supply to "punish" him or her.

You would be surprised at the number of husbands sleeping sulkily month after month on the sofa out in the hall—or in the guest bedroom. You would be surprised at the number of wives with luscious figures whose husbands haven't made love to them for months—or years.

In helping married couples click together, some of the most beautiful women I have personologized had been ignored physically by their husbands for a long time, and were eating their hearts out. Maybe these women didn't like sex as such, but they did like being loved and noticed.

One of the best illustrations along this line was in the

movie, "Rear Window." The news photographer who had broken his leg (a role played by James Stewart) was convalescing in the back apartment of a large building, and his rear window faced the back windows of opposite apartments. He had a nose for news, and while waiting for his broken leg to heal, noticed many things through the open windows facing him. He even solved one murder. But in a different apartment he noticed a young woman he called "The Torso" for obvious reasons. She let men bring her home but successfully sidestepped each anxious escort at the door—no one ever got into her apartment. She was waiting for her G-I husband to return.

But when her soldier did arrive home after his long absence, he didn't do first what you would expect. He had a trait for liking food. He went to the refrigerator, took out a carton of food and the makings of a feast, and settled himself down alone for a leisurely repast—while his beautiful wife waited!

You have to understand personology to believe such a thing could happen. But people are built so differently that there really could be a man with such a build. However, most men are built more like the ski trooper who, on arriving home after his long stint in the service, was so anxious that the *second* thing he did was take off his skis.

Usually men and women try hard to do their part in marriage. I remember a Navy wife waiting for her husband's return, who spent considerable time at the dentist's just so her teeth would look beautiful for him. And she was attractive to start with.

After the novelty of having the other partner available for sex wears off, the husband and wife both have to watch out for their other traits, or these will get in the way of lovemaking.

161

Men are generally more mechanical about sex than women, more hungry for it and less deterred by lack of optimum conditions. In personology statistics they are also usually found to be coarser, more earthy, more cynical, less emotional and less idealistic.

The main thing to remember about the sex drive is that no trait operates in a vacuum (with either husband or wife). These traits must be considered in approaching any love partner. Husband and wife each want to be approached like a human being and not like an automobile.

Husbands are pleasantly surprised at how well their wives respond to sex when they approach the woman FIRST AS AN INDIVIDUAL, a unique and worthwhile person in her own right—and SECONDLY as a female.

The key to approaching anyone is the key trait involved for that particular person. Naturally, since people are as different as their fingerprints, it varies with each individual.

Let us look at it from the woman's standpoint. My wife Elizabeth, a successful wife and mother, is an experienced personologist who has helped countless couples save their marriages. She says:

The thin-skinned woman married to a thicker-skinned husband will often fight the foreplay and demand that her husband not have sex except at long intervals. When a woman fights, the fluids of the vagina dry up . . . and that is what makes sex so uncomfortable for the thin-skinned. She will become irritable all during the day in anticipation of the possibility of sex. Love can only thrive under positive vibrations. This is why the finely-textured woman has such a difficult time adjusting to sex. She will say, "If I never have sex again, it will be too soon." She needs to be loved delicately. No word of sex should be given until the couple is behind closed doors, alone. The fine-textured woman's tissues are so thin that they shrink with any distasteful emotion. Then sex hurts the tissues. She needs a certain amount of plain love before sex, to get her released, so that the couple can enjoy sex together.

The husband must just *love* his fine-textured wife sometimes without sex. They must lie in each other's arms, or play music together . . . but that music has to be melodic and harmonious. She is the one who needs refined surroundings, beautiful clothing, and delicate foods. She is expensive. She likes jewelry and furs, candles, and everything that is refined, and in small amounts at a time.

If you are a fine-textured woman, you realize that you can respond and let go fully in sex if you are approached properly, and make up your mind that you are willing to enter the act.

The thick-skinned, rugged woman can stand more of the coarseness of sex, but she needs a vigorous approach and vigorous stimulation. And she needs time to come to her climax. She will often not have her climax . . . so she will need to be prepared longer so that both she and her husband can share it.

The soft body-tone wife will respond to her partner more quickly. The hard body-tone wife is less responsive, but she is very sincere and genuine when she does respond. Not too many women are hard. They respond fully when they do respond. They are often impatient earlier —but if they remember that their act of sex is more satisfying to them than to the softer person, they need only see their sex act complete in their mind, and then stay with sex as long as they need. If they want to become softer and more quickly responsive, some of the things that help are to shower with a hard spray, drink lots of fruit juices instead of liquor, and generally relax. Liquor at first accelerates the need for sex . . . later it takes away the ability.

163

The wife with high emotionality (and the large eyes) wants love before sex. She wants understanding and no criticism. When an affectionate wife's feelings are hurt, she cannot respond as well as usual. Of course, she must have dominion over herself. But what is said to her about sex must be constructive and positive. She can be an excellent partner in sex when she and her husband understand themselves. Her husband's tone of voice will mean everything to her.

The wife who has low emotionality (and small eyes) will tend to refuse to express love before or after sex. She has a job to do, and she does it. She must learn never to argue or criticize . . . and to give her partner what he needs before she gets what she needs. She can compliment her mate on how well he has done something, and she can put her arms around him gently and smile.

The husband of the undemonstrative wife needs to understand that it is hard for her to be affectionate. He must know that he is loved by her as much as she can show it.

The wife who is critical (her eyes slant down at the outside) must remember that she must never criticize her mate except to point out something GOOD about him. He must do the same for her. This trait of criticism can prevent a lot of lovemaking. Either husband or wife can get into a frame of mind where they do not want to make love because they were criticized.

The uncritical wife (characterized by eyes slanting up at the outer corners) has less of a problem. But she must be alert to what her husband needs, and be willing to provide it. She is poor at evaluating situations, but she is not a nag.

The woman with low tolerance (whose eyes are close together) gets angry if her husband does not return in time for dinner . . . or if he does not do what she wants him to, promptly . . . then she will have nothing to do with him—she will have no sex with him, until he does what she wants him to. He should avoid doing anything that will make her at all jealous. (Whenever a woman is upset, the membranes of her vagina and uterus dry, and sex hurts her . . . so there must be much more time in preparation for sex.)

The woman with the high tolerance (whose eyes are far apart) often gets criticized because she does not have meals on time . . . or that she does not come to bed on time. Her husband must not criticize before sex. He can tell her when he wants food. And he can beg her to come to bed with him.

The woman with a large ego (with the broad face) married to a man with a smaller ego, often discourages him—and especially when he is having difficulty with sex, as when he fears he is becoming impotent. For example, one woman chewed apples and nuts while her husband was attempting to perform, and drove him wild. A man has to concentrate on sex, not on reactions to his wife.

The large-ego wife talks to her husband about what he should do about sex, during the relationship—she will say she is only trying to help him. But he has to perform accordingly as he is made. She disturbs him before sex by being more self-confident than he is . . . and suggesting to him that he work more . . . that he have larger goals . . . that he earn more money—all of which discourages him. She acts more like a mother than a wife.

Actually, she should take an extra job herself outside the home, with no conversation about it nor the job of her husband, unless he wants to confide in her. And if he asks her what he should do, she should say, "Well, since you ask me, this is what I think you should do . . . but I know that you will do the right thing." This is the way she should show her faith in him.

In sex, she should say nothing about how he should approach her, but just let him do whatever he likes—and thank him for it! If he seems to have difficulty in accomplishing the sex act, she can encourage him afterwards by saying, "You will be able to have sex—see yourself in your mind completing sex before you start." And after a few times, he will find that he can. But, they too must remain good friends, and be loving toward each other, in any instance of difficulty.

If the woman has a small ego (narrow-faced) she must follow the lead of her man. She must know that she must give him satisfaction or he wouldn't have married her. If she pictures the consummation of sex she will accomplish her role . . . and know that she will always be up to having sex with him whenever he wants. She must be more thorough in everything she does, and keep her mind on finishing her part of things, instead of her reaction to things.

The man with a wife with a small ego should always express love to his wife, and never demand sex of her before she has had time to visualize it in her mind. In sex he should compliment her upon what she does well—then suggest the next step for her to learn . . . after which he will take over. It takes about a year for this trait to grow —but if he will be content with one step of progress at a time, he will have dominion over this situation of his wife's timidity.

The aloof or discriminating wife (indicated by eyebrows set high above the pupil of the eyes) dislikes to consider sex outside the bedroom. So the husband must learn not to talk about it, nor to pat her on her buttocks, but to only do things for her that she wants done . . . to smile at her, to talk pleasantly . . . Then when the bedroom door is closed, he can do what he wants. But he still must always be in good taste. She likes privacy and can respond best when there is nobody around except her husband.

The affable wife (with eyebrows sitting down close to the eyes) is apt to offend her husband if he is discriminative, by touching him frequently, or talking to him about sex in front of others . . . or by her having loose relationships with other men. She tends to talk over her problems or listen to other persons' problems, and gets suckered into relationships which her husband cannot accept. The affable wife may be quite dainty but she can prepare for sex right in front of her husband, whereas the discriminating wife cannot stand to do that.

The wife with large lips is generous. But she is not concise, and she wants longer preparation for sex, or she feels that her husband does not like her. With her taking more time for sex, she also needs understanding for her taking longer to get to bed . . . and for her doing more things for other people during the day than she does for her own family. (So there are always things her husband could complain about, like undone chores.) She must discipline herself to a definite bedtime. But because of her generous outpouring nature, her husband will probably forgive her for a great many such foibles.

The wife who has small lips is the concise individual. She wants sex quickly and efficiently, with little time for play. She often offends by her use of nouns and verbs without adjectives and adverbs. So the husband should approach her at a definite convenient time, without talking too much about sex.

The wife with a hump on her nose (administrative or business-like) knows the value of the sex relationship. She will have a tendency to be more willing for sex when she wants something. She does not have the ability to react quickly to the other person's wants. Over a period of time, if her husband does not produce what she wants him to produce in the way of a living, she may refuse him sex.

The ministrative wife (with a straight or dipped nose) wants to help. So she will have the least difficulty in sex. She thinks only of the other person and his needs . . . and tries to satisfy him.

The wife who is round-headed and conserving is the homemaker. She will appreciate sex like food. She can settle down and enjoy.

The constructive wife (the square-headed mesomorph) is going to appreciate sex quite differently, as a part of her business routine. This is why so many marriages that fail have wives or husbands with the trait of construction. The constructive wife must always remember that it is her husband who needs sex. And since she promised to comfort him (in the marriage ceremony) she will do so. Over a period of time she will often have occasion to be reminded of this, when she would rather sew or even scrub the floor. She is job-minded.

The wife with worry lines between her eyebrows is exacting and fussy. She will be negative if her husband skips any steps. She will often be thinking of things that she had to do before sex, so her mind is cluttered. She must learn to expect every moment to be a new moment, and to adjust as well as she can. Her husband must carry through his regime of sex without being upset by her fussiness.

The wife with detail-concern (with the burdened brow) never wants sex out of order, until she has finished what she is doing. She cannot leave her work easily. So, her mate had best let her take care of details before he approaches her.

The methodical wife, with the ledge above her brows, does not want anyone to tell her what to do or when to do it—nor to interfere with her once she has started. So her man had best suggest sex when he knows that she has finished what she has been doing. He deserves extra credit if he can get her to try some new approach or some new method of lovemaking.

The aesthetic wife has straight eyebrows. She wants all things to be in harmony. She will have to have a clean bed and comfortable covering in a well-decorated room. She must be approached first through loving and then she will fulfill her sex role. She will want sex to be well-arranged and quietly accomplished. Her husband should particularly avoid any arguments at preceding times of the day.

The dramatic wife has high sweeping arched eyebrows. She will

168

want special gowns or jewelry or music, as a stage setting for sex. She is always on stage, and will over react to right or wrong things that are done. She has to learn to keep quiet while her husband has sex with her, so that she does encourage him instead of discourage him.

The wife with magnetism has a smile in the eye. She must learn to always smile at her husband when he wants sex. If she smiles at other men, and not at her husband, she will offend him. Men will want to flirt with her. She can be a lot of fun.

If your wife has glassy eyes, she has fugacity . . . so do not expect her to respond too well to you. Give her a drink of fruit juice to help her settle down and relax before sex. Avoid anything that might make her upset or argumentative . . . she already feels there are too many things she does not have in hand. On her part, she should relax and be glad to have sex with her partner.

The wife who is melancholy has white showing under the colored part of her eyes. She is either tired or under pressure . . . or has some problem she is unhappy or worried about. She particularly needs love and reassurance. Her husband should expect her to talk pretty gloomily and he should not be upset about it. She should make herself appreciative of her mate's good points, and should think of pleasing him.

The wife whose corners of the mouth turn upward is optimistic . . . and will be a more cheerful partner in sex. She will always have the feeling that sex will be better as time goes on.

The wife whose lips turn down is pessimistic and can never see anything good in an act of sex (or anything else in life!). She must not talk during sex, because being pessimistic she would talk negatively. Her husband should keep his mind on what he is doing, knowing that her negative speech has nothing to do with her loving him.

Again, remember that no trait operates in a vacuum, and there may be some balancing combinations of traits. The fine-textured wife dislikes coarseness, but she may go along with it better for being affable and affectionate and ministrative. The husband should try, however, to bear her native daintiness in mind, in approaching her.

Love means an emotional attachment. Two people want to kiss each other, fondle each other. In other words, love between two individuals is more than the relationship between brother and sister. Two people who are very much in love, still cannot always enjoy sex without dominion over themselves. Personology, the science of individual structural variation and functioning, believes that sex is the last step of love . . . and involves dominion over the individual's native makeup.

The wife whose interest is more in things than in people, must learn never to argue. She should just say her part of the conversation once, and then follow the leader . . . she must give him a chance to make the decision.

Stubbornness is one trait which affects the marriage relationship greatly. The woman is most often the culprit. She gets angry at her husband's treatment of her, or something that is said to her. Then she decides, in retaliation, that she will refuse sex. The husband cannot understand, and will often get acquainted with someone else. The wife must realize that stubbornness must be used only to see what SHE must do . . . and she must always remember that regardless of her feelings about anything else, sex is one thing that she should give to her husband whenever he wants it. Perhaps then he won't be as critical of her.

To the woman, sex is not as mechanical as it is to a man. So the wife must remember that her man does need her. As she gives sex to him willingly, he will not need it as often, because he no longer has to prove that he is acceptable and important.

The direction in which a relationship is going is important—

whether the man and wife are growing closer together or drifting apart. There are traits by which a person may resentfully start sleeping in a separate bed. One couple had this happen. The wife was suddenly awakened by a roar of thunder and, frightened, ran and jumped into her husband's arms before she thought. They hadn't been close for months. But then they were close immediately, and the feud was over. See to it that it doesn't take a thunderstorm to keep you and your spouse in the same bed.

Thank you, Mrs. Whiteside.

Now let us think again from the man's point of view. Some men are so abashed by their wife's larger ego that they are impotent in HER presence. They are afraid of her in the dining room, and they are afraid of her in the bedroom. Or, she may be intolerant, and he may be fed up with her constant complaining and want no part of her.

An example: One ship's master had separated from his wife. They argued so much that he had no interest in her as a person, and in her presence was impotent. But he could get an erection if some other woman so much as touched his hand, or a waitress brushed up against him. He was built coarsely and matter-of-fact. Pictures showed that his wife was thin-skinned and emotional. I coached him to approach her with finesse and with round-the-clock warmth and lovingness. He went back to her, and his manhood was restored the very first night. His being a man again meant so much to him that he later brought me as a present a fine clock made abroad.

Men, as well as women, have traits. Usually the man is the more aggressive partner. And *he* biologically never has to worry about getting pregnant. But sometimes he, as a person, has the weaker traits in some area and needs some encouragement from his wife.

The wider-faced, large-ego wife, has to watch out or she will make her narrower-faced husband feel not needed. She will act very self-sufficient unless she is alert about this trait; she may get into a mother role instead of a sweetheart role. She may throw him right into the arms of some other woman who has perhaps a poorer figure, but who builds him up.

How does the other woman get him? She doesn't necessarily wear a bikini and wiggle her breasts in front of him. She looks worshipfully into his eyes. She smiles and is fun. She asks his help and advice. She tells him how proud of him she is for how well he handled the boss when the boss flew in from the home office. She makes him feel ten feet tall. Every time he thinks about her, he glows.

If his broad-faced wife wants to hold her narrow-faced husband in the face of competition, the rule of thumb is for her to act around him the very same way the other woman would act who was trying to get her meat hooks into him and get him away from her! And she really knows what to do, if she will only get her traits out of the way and apply herself.

In the sexual area (as in other areas of human relationship) the key always is: *Work on your own trait and talk to the other person's.*

13. CHILDREN

Your children's genetic programming is complete. They have all the traits a grown-up has—they are just learning to direct them.

If your child is analytical, whether he is preschool or teen-ager, explain WHY before you make a request. Then he's happy to do it. If your child is ministrative, get around his stubbornness by asking him to help. If he is warm and emotional, he needs a hug or a wink. If he has a strong, broad-faced nature, be prepared: He feels the strength of his nature and is likely to announce what he chooses to do, himself, instead of doing what you tell him. He does not respect weakness. Have fun with him, but keep clear in his mind who's in charge.

If your child is thin-skinned and silky-haired, he is more sensitive and delicate, more liable to be picky about his food. Give him his nourishment in smaller helpings attractively served, to get him started.

If he is soft and whiney, see he toughens up. Don't let him work you by the "tyranny of weakness." Have him follow through on what he does. Get him to become more ready to face the world.

173

Children have face language, too. You don't have to be much of a personologist to recognize that the large eyes of this child spell affection and the need to be loved . . . and that the expression is one of interest and concern about the situation and how the child fits into it. Here is a little girl with sympathy, helpfulness and responsiveness . . . loving but discriminative, not wanting to be picked up and held by just anybody . . . and with more mental concern than physical activity.

What a delight a youngster can be who is accommodating, glad to help, and who has a generous disposition! You can bypass stubbornness if you appeal to traits such as these.

174

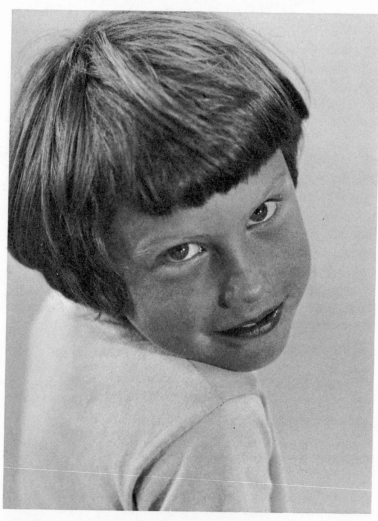

What sort of boy is this? Without face language, you just say, "An intriguing child." But with face language, you recognize that this boy is a very balanced personality. He is fun to be around, but you can deal with him just as with an adult, as far as intelligently discussing situations and reasons. He is intelligent. He likes to understand reasons and causes. He has a fair tolerance, so that he will want to do the right thing without being either intolerant and petty, or too lax and easygoing. He has plenty of courage and self-confidence. He will be thorough in using his toys, such as in building a fort and deploying toy soldiers. With his balance, he is still forceful and will work hard to make things happen . . . and to happen his way, because he is self-reliant. He is also adventurous and stubborn. With him you use reason to keep him gladly moving ahead.

Brothers and sisters have personalities, along with individualities. Here you will recognize a dramatic young person who means what he says and carries through . . . who is trusting and helpful. He is quick to speak. He is an all-out individual who, once involved, goes all the way. He likes to be where the action is, and to be a part of it. His sister (left) is on the modest side in her opinion of herself, seldom finds fault, is a direct person rather than one who cross-examines you about all the reasons. She expects others to make the first move in getting acquainted—but she likes to entertain, has a knack with food, and loves her home. . . . She also likes to go places and do things, and has an artistic bent.

Every youngster is just as much an individual as each adult. If you were going to deal with this young man, he would be much more interesting to you, and you would click far better with him, if you used your face-language to realize that he is quite intelligent. Talk to him just as you would to an adult, insofar as grasping subject matter goes. Be aware that he likes to know the reasons for things, being analytical. Your tone of voice should be warm, because he is on the affectionate side. He has quite a bit of courage, so be direct with him, as long as you are friendly. He is however, critical, and will be quick to notice your flaws or inconsistencies.

If he's hard and tough, be firm with him so you know it registers. If he's broad between the eyes, he takes a broad view and nothing seems very immediate or pressing. He puts things off. Spot-check him to make sure he does his studies. Give him a two-minute warning when it's time to come to the table.

If he's close between the eyes, he's hard to please and quick to point out where YOU weren't perfect. (You have scrubbed the whole kitchen floor, and he points to one spot and says, "You didn't get this one.") Explain to him that he must perfect himself first, before he worries about how anyone else is doing.

If he has laugh lines at the outer edges of the eyes, you can kid with him easily and have jokes and fun with him. If his rhetoric lines are developing, let him read to you while you are doing the ironing or waxing the car, as the case may be. You grow closer together with anyone by doing things with him.

The above suggestions also work with girls. Traits are no respecters of gender.

Will Rogers said, "You have to be smart to be a horseman. You have to know more than a horse." The same idea applies to children. Over the narrow genetic bridge, they have inherited a lot of qualities from you, a lot of strong equipment. Give them boundaries, the same as adults, so they know where they stand. Give them supervised activities, so they can have the benefit of your coaching and experience, and your love and support.

Eye-contact is extremely important with children, as well as adults. That's why it pays off to go around in front of your child when he is about to dash outdoors, put a hand on each shoulder, look in his eyes, and see that he looks in yours, before telling him what time you want him to be back. If you just yell it at him as he dashes out he may say, "Yes, Mom" or "Yes, Dad," but it hasn't really registered.

Talk to your child's most salient trait, and you have the key to maintaining a close relationship. If he has the narrow face of the self-conscious child, be especially sure to keep your voice down. And do not frighten him by telling him at one time about many things he has to do.

With small children, two of the most important traits to watch are emotionality and texture. The emotional child particularly needs a lot of love and caressing. The thin-skinned child is sensitive physically and needs extra protection against the environment or climate.

With teen-agers, judgment traits and patterns of responsibility are important. The child broad between the eyes, who was such an adorable good-natured baby, now is getting out more into his own world—and his tolerant attitude of "all right, anything goes" can get him into all kinds of trouble.

You will find that if you talk traits to your child (and teach him some face language) you can more easily avoid making him feel put down or not trusted. Say, "That easy-going build of yours makes us all love you, but please do make it easier for yourself by not getting behind in your studies." By this approach, you can show him that you like him as a person—that it is just the pesky trait which has to be kept in line. In this way you are not put in the position of rejecting him as a total person. Like a good football coach, you are just showing him how he can learn to do something better.

Your children will be interested when you point out to them, through face language, an outstanding quality about a friend or teacher. You will be helping them learn to approach the world of individuals in such a way that they will take an attitude of expecting each individual to be naturally different instead of all the same—each a special person instead of a generality. This will prevent a lot of difficulty and heartbreak, and bring success more quickly.

You will notice that you cannot see the upper eyelid of this youngster. The fold covering the upper eyelid is the indicator of analyticalness—of liking to know the reasons and figure things out (which is a factor in his thoughtful expression). To such a person, you always should explain all the reasons "why."

181

14. MONEY

In dealing with others about matters of money, it will pay you to remember the Chinese axiom that the man with the hook or convex nose looks out for himself financially and is hard to handle. Also, he perks up at a bargain, and wants to get his money's worth. He likes to pay his own way and not be under obligation.

"Specials" in the supermarket, and "deals," like getting an extra supply of gasoline with the car you buy, appeal to the man or woman with the Roman nose. Ordinarily they know to the dollar how much money they have in the bank. Their checks are less liable to bounce.

Ask the administrative, hump-nosed individual where the best places are to shop. He knows. He comes to life when talking about them.

Your financial advisor has more on the ball if he has this administrative, commercial build. To him, money talks. He really rolls out the red carpet for his best customers.

If you are hiring a bookkeeper, hire one with a hump on the nose. You will notice he or she ENJOYS keeping track of money. Usually this person is also better at arithmetic, for the figures mean something, especially if they represent money.

You will notice that the woman with a Roman nose is often talking about prices and money. If your wife has this build, you can trust her to write the checks. At least let her write the routine checks, such as for gas and electricity. She will enjoy doing it, and will do it well. She will keep the stubs filled out, and the balance accurate.

One wife had such a pronounced score on this trait that she suggested her husband tip her each time they made love. He always left a five dollar bill under the pillow on her side of the bed. (Few women are this mercenary.)

But any Roman-nosed wife brightens up if she is given extra money to spend for which she does not have to account to her husband. She will make good use of that money, too. She is penny-wise. (Building security in the long run involves other traits.)

The Roman-nosed individual takes more interest in a budget, and is more liable to stick to it. He (or she) also likes to take on a share of the financial burden, such as by contributing to the expenses on a trip, or paying the proper tip.

One commercially-minded woman was generous, so she donated her services to a church, as the organist. But her feelings were hurt because the church officials did not pay her parking fee.

If you are selecting a purchasing agent or someone who sets prices, it will pay you to choose the one with the commercial nose.

Should you yourself lack this quality, utilize the commercial trait vicariously by consulting a Roman-nosed or hawk-nosed person about prices you should set, or fees you should charge.

Also, if you lack the businesslike build, take more pride in getting paid for what you do, and in being able to pay for what you get. Save money so you can do what you would like to do. Change jobs if the competing employer will pay you more. Pay more attention to money. Cultivate people who have money.

Doug Pledger said: "Money isn't important. It's just the people who have it who are!"

If you lack the thrift trait, develop saving habits so that you accumulate. A handy rule is to save 10 percent of what you earn, and live off the other 90 percent.

One man who became well-to-do, started by carrying around $4.00 he had earned, to attract more money. The four dollar bills represented money he had earned working extra hours or doing something hard for him, such as walking to save bus money. He refused any temptation to spend his magnet-money. This kept him in the frame of mind to keep accumulating.

Another trait which has much to do with your finances is the quality of generosity or its opposite, conciseness. The full-lipped person is the automatic giver—liberal in pouring out whatever he has. The person with tight, small, hard lips is less generous—he does not automatically give, but can direct his spending . . . he will give only to his dear ones, ordinarily. Don't expect your tight-lipped uncle to finance your new business enterprise, unless you provide adequate security. (If you can prove you don't need money, he may be willing to lend you some!)

If you yourself have bulbous lips, work all the harder to control your generosity if you want to get ahead financially. Don't be a soft-touch. Be liberal to yourself first. Have the

As serious as a person's mien may seem at the moment, try him out and you will find that if he is the affable sort, easily approachable. The physical indicator in this instance is the manner in which the eyebrows sit close to the eyes. Here is a man who is sincere and analytical, but far from stuffy, . . . he can be approached informally (and he can make friends easily.)

training, advantages, equipment, resources, money and rest which put you in the position of being able to do more. You cannot help others unless you are better off than they are. Stop feeling guilty about treating yourself as well as you would expect your cousin to treat himself.

Think twice before you volunteer a loan. The least you should require of yourself is to see that anything you hand out was your *own* idea . . . that someone did not come along and press your hot-button of generosity. Follow the law of overflow: Be true to yourself first. If you have time and energy and resources left, then do something for your family. If you still have an overflow, your friends come next. Only after that, worry about giving any of your hard-earned savings to those with less priority. Generally, be generous with the spirit rather than the substance.

People are more liable to appreciate what they themselves have earned. As the dentists say, "It's the teeth that are paid for that fit best." Or, as a Utah personologist put it, "Don't borrow trouble—borrow money, and trouble will follow!"

And . . . in case you have a temporary emergency or have an opportunity and do have to borrow, now you know the person who is most likely to lend the money to you—the person with the concave (ski-jump) nose and full lips.

15. EVERYDAY SITUATIONS

Use your smile freely at the breakfast table, not only to be cheery and popular with others at the table, but to keep up your own good vibrations. And even before breakfast, "hit the deck" cheerfully, to get the day off to a good start. If you have an easygoing, broad-viewed nature, jump out of bed when you first hear the alarm go off. If you are soft and inclined to be whiney, shake it off by a cold shower—that will help toughen you up and make sure that your own face language is "bright-eyed and bushy-tailed" as you start the day.

Should your mate be large-eyed and affectionate, take the time to cuddle and hug and kiss, and say a sweet word, when waking him or her up. If your mate is methodical, have everything ready and in place which is involved with preparing for the day.

At the breakfast table, you can kid with anyone who has the sunny laugh lines of humor extending outward from the outside corners of the eyes. If someone at the table is gloomy-eyed, at first go a little easy on gaiety until you can help him or her get more in the mood. There is a law of layers, like melting ice, and you can lead the other person only a layer at a time.

If the others involved are close between the eyes and hard to please, fit in better with them by having things done on time. Expect some complaints but don't take them seriously. Figure that's just part of life-with-a-perfectionist. Remember it's just the other person's trait, and has nothing to do with whether that person loves you. Listen respectfully, and after due passage of time so you don't seem to be changing the subject, talk cheerily about something pleasant.

The best way to win a battle is not to have one. Watch the other's eyes (with friendly interest) and you'll be cued better into the momentary mood. If there's a frowning look, and it's almost time to dash for the bus, skip any suggestion right then and there about an extra errand. Eyes can tell you a lot. It will be wonderful when telephones have a television apparatus attached so that you can see the face language of the person to whom you are talking.

Be especially alert at "turning points," when one activity ends and it is time to start the next . . . and to the ATTITUDE with which it is started. Particularly watch face language when someone enters the room or is about to leave it. By looking up bright-eyed and giving a pleasant "Hi!" or "So long!," you make a lot of points with the other individual, especially if that person has the large eyes of the warm and sentimental.

In your situations during the day, lips are important to observe, also. If the other person has large, loose lips, expect him or her to do a lot of talking. Budget your time accordingly. You know that if that full-mouthed individual sticks a nose in the door and says, "I just want to talk to you for a minute," that it will probably take 15. Enjoy it, and patiently listen.

Time-giving will average out because of the briefer periods

you need to spend with tight-mouthed, thin-lipped individuals. These people always seem to be in a hurry to get on to the next thing. (If you are in a hurry for service, pick out the tight-mouthed clerk with thin lips—if you want a favor done, choose a clerk with full lips, a concave ministrative nose, and broadness between the eyes.)

Face language will give you handles to use in clicking even better with people you already know. Take a fresh look at your neighbor. Then talk to the key trait. If the eyes are large, talk about the family, dear ones, mutual friends, old times, happy occasions. If the nose is aristocratic, ask advice about prices or shopping.

Some of the most expressive language is nonverbal. The cool glance of the person next to you on the bus or plane tells you to go easy on forcing conversation. Or, a friendly glance tells you that the person would be willing to help hold a package for you while you get organized. If you miss such obvious cues as these, you have only yourself to blame.

Remember that not only is a smile a handy lubricant in daily episodes—it is also a good way to test the mood of other people, by the degree of their response. Try a smile, for openers. Even with the discriminative, high-browed individual, it is likely to bring a response . . . and start breaking the ice.

Face language has introduced you to the World of Individuals. You recognize that each person you encounter is unique in his or her own right. Your eyes and expression are more genuinely interested and friendly . . . and more alert and personable, for noticing others more specifically. Others need recognition, and you stand out in their mind because you are

How much more interesting your face-language knowledge makes people! There's a lot of personality in this picture, for example. Magnetism, of course—lots of it! A gift for words. A feeling for the dramatic. Ability at oral self-expression. Courage. And some somberness in the eyes, balanced by a rich sense of humor. And an expanding sense of confidence in his abilities. Such a vital personality to deal with! A rather demanding personality, but you would know, in dealing with him, which buttons to press, so to speak.

190

giving them more recognition than others. They are inclined toward you in a friendly way.

You also know the danger signs of when to tread lightly. You know this from the expression of the moment—and you also know what to anticipate. If the other person has glassy eyes, he or she is on edge, and might do almost anything unexpected or inefficient. If the other person is critical, be on your best behavior or you will encounter some fault-finding. In many situations in life, it is not what you do so much as *how* you do it. Your goals are probably sound ones, but it is in the manner of how you proceed toward these goals (in the world of individuals) that you have to be alert.

16. IN THE OFFICE

Statistics show that most of the people who are fired from their jobs are terminated not because of lack of ability to do the work, but because of personality difficulties or lack of cooperation.

What is *your* face language like in the office? Do you get across to your superior your willingness to cooperate? Or are you like the people who get laid off when the opportunity comes, because they *show* no alacrity to get things done or to get someone else's idea (even if on the inside they *are* willing).

You know some people who are popular with management who are no whiz on their job, and who even show up late and get by with it. Even if their performance is mediocre, at least they get across their idea of being *willing*.

Of course, anyone reading this book has more ambition than the average individual, or you wouldn't be trying to improve yourself, and perform more effectively. So if you will steer your traits well and get that inner spirit across as well as using your native talents vocationally, more and more things will come up roses.

Think of the people you know who are popular at work. They greet not only you pleasantly, but everyone. They are

Everything must be in good taste for this young woman. She is selective and discriminative. But once she chooses, she is all-out and thorough along the direction she takes. She is affectionate, generous, sympathetic and sincere.

optimistic. They use their smile freely. They are friendly and give you full focus with their eyes when they are talking with you or listening to you. They have magnetism and live eyes.

In statistical procedure, there is a way of using large-number statistical methods when you have passed the 29 mark in the size of the group. So if you have that large a number of people with whom you work, there's a lot of variety in those individuals. Some will naturally click with you, because they are more your build. But you get no credit for getting along well with them. You get credit only for making friends of those who are not your natural cup of tea, so to speak. You will find yourself using your face language knowledge most with the people who are most difficult for you to deal with.

One young man was located where he could personally get a full-fledged personological analysis, and learn some face language so he could understand himself and others better. He was promoted so rapidly with a major transportation company that he was placed in charge of men with much greater seniority. One of the men over whose head he had been vaulted was angry at him, and made a point of giving the young man a rough time in all possible ways. The rising young executive came back to talk to me. I asked him to describe the man who was being nasty to him . . . and found that the older man had a narrow face and evidently was self-conscious and upset. The younger man followed advice to be pleasant and casual around the older man, and whenever possible complimented him . . . but proceeded only a step at a time in making friends . . . first of all, to get across his *attitude* of liking the older man. The situation relaxed and they became the best of friends.

Who is the one at work who can promote you? Take a

3×5 card and jot down that person's salient features. Then look back in the earlier sections of this book to the appropriate suggestions on what to do in approaching someone with those traits. Put that knowledge to work and gain the corresponding results.

If you want to be really thorough, check your own traits in relation to your superior's key traits. If he is tight-lipped and you are mouthy, you'll suddenly fit in with him much better if you get into projects faster with less talking. If he's affectionate, ask him at coffee break how the youngsters are doing.

Fitting in with the other person's build when around him is not two-faced . . . any more than it is hypocritical to get a ladder when you need to change a light bulb in a high ceiling. With face language, you can stop resenting doing what you always knew would work, but which you once considered apple-polishing. This does not mean that you are to give in on a matter of principle. But such situations are rare. No matter how pretty the secretary, it's seldom the boss who's chasing her around the table.

17. SELLING

"I have doubled my sales since learning how to tell what individuals are like," an Oakland, California woman who has learned physical indicators of personality told me recently.

"How is that?" I asked.

"I *listen* to the other person instead of talking so much myself like I used to," replied the saleswoman. She has full lips, and is inclined toward the verbose.

A Redwood City, California district sales manager for one of the great insurance companies has studied the personological approach. He announced last week at a lecture I gave that the men he has chosen and trained each earn an average of $10,000 a year MORE than other men in similar positions for the same company.

If you pay attention to your own build and play up your strong points, and if you approach the other person the way he is constituted individually, your efficiency in selling goes up. So does your enjoyment of selling.

Even a small trait like detail-concern can pay off when noticed. A Tracy, California real estate salesman earned $27,000 the year before he took a face language sales course, and $62,000 the following year.

196

"In selling homesites," he said, "if I notice the prospects have the knobby brows of detail-concern, I show them every little cotton-picking rock on the whole acreage . . . and they eat it up. If they have large eyes, I talk about how the kids will love having a home of their own."

Top honors for using structure/function knowledge round the clock, though, might very well go to the successful Danville, California wife (and mother of seven children—six daughters and the "miracle") who netted $23,000 on the side with the sale of beauty products and food supplements, besides doing a great job with her family. She can sell quicker because through noticing what trait to talk to, she doesn't have to go through her whole sales speech. She knows right away what strong point about her product will make that individual sale. And she herself looks so young that when she went to the wedding of one of her older daughters, people asked, "Where's the mother of the bride?"

You save a lot of nervous energy if you realize that the other people with whom you're dealing are each built differently. Knowing how people are different by nature is more valuable in a one-to-one situation than knowing how human beings as a whole are similar.

A Salt Lake City, Utah door-to-door salesman learned face language. He had his own complete personological analysis performed. Among other things, he found out that by nature he was more on the timid side, and needed to build his self-confidence and be more audacious. You might say he was too much like the collie and not enough like the bulldog. He began to notice other people's faces, and his sales soared. His instructor asked him, "What are you doing differently?"

From your face language, you know that this man is friendly and can be kidded . . . that he nevertheless is critical and analytical (that he will see flaws, and he has to know "why") . . . that he is on the genuine and sincere side . . . that he has an excellent vocabulary and appreciates words well used . . . that he is exacting and wants things just right . . . that he is conscious of every detail . . . and that he is free of melancholy, has nothing major on his mind, and is free of pressure. That's a lot more than you would know without face language.

"Well," he answered, "I find that if I meet another person who has a face as narrow or narrower than mine, I can sell him. I concentrate on that kind. I don't waste my time. But when I ring the doorbell and a broad-faced man answers, I say, "Oh, excuse me, I have come to the wrong address!"

One reason I do so much traveling is the spectacular success life insurance salesmen have had whom I have personologized. Working with the staff of one of the largest companies, I have coached men from New York to Honolulu, and from Minneapolis to Corpus Christi.

With an insurance agency, my procedure is usually first to give a lecture instructing the men (and women) in the key face language traits of prospective clients. Then I personologize them individually. I coach them on their strong points and how to best utilize them. Also, I am frank about their weak points and how to build them up. I make a tape recording that they can play back from time to time, to keep sharp, and on the up-swing in their unfoldment of their capacities to full potential. Also, they get a graph outlining their qualities in regard to 68 factors.

I have found it is valuable for salesmen to sell (when they have a choice) to others of their own kind. Such people click together.

I told a Chicago life insurance salesman I analyzed that he scored high on the dramatic trend, and that he should be able to sell well to show-people. That night he was watching a broadcast, and noticed how dramatic the television master of ceremonies was. When the broadcast ended at 11 p.m., he phoned the emcee and got an appointment to see him the next day. He sold him life insurance. Since then he has sold many of the emcee's friends and associates. And he enjoys dealing with that kind of people. Not only are they his breed, but it is of interest to him to talk over with them their activities and their plans—because he could have done the very same thing, as one of his own diverse possible vocations.

18. CRIME

Has your home ever been burglarized? It makes you angry to have your privacy invaded, your precious keepsakes pawed over and many of them stolen. And all this while you were away, so you never got a look at the thief. You know, since 85 percent of the burglaries are committed by drug addicts (according to the California attorney general), that the thief probably had unnatural eyes, and certainly no free and open gaze. He was after anything he could sell for a quick fix.

But as you read the headlines and watch the television newscasts, you realize that there are much more horrifying crimes than burglaries. Senseless murders top the list. I recall that when I was a child in Madera, California, our family had a friend, a blind man. Sightless as he was, he earned his living by operating a popcorn and peanut wagon he rolled around by hand. One morning we were horrified to learn that our blind friend, on his way home the night before from his stand in front of the theatre, had been beaten to death by someone with a hammer.

As a grown man, I became a news editor, and reported crimes of many natures. Then when I changed vocations and entered the structure/function field, I did research at the world's largest prison. By that time, I knew enough physical indicators of individual tendencies that I never needed to ask an inmate what his offense had been. It was apparent by the time his analysis was completed, whether it was a crime of emotion and passion, spontaneous or planned, and whether it had to do with money or grudges.

The eyes, of course, are the best indicators. The hardened killer has steely eyes . . . eyes inclined to focus beyond you. He has turned his back on his best self. He has taken human life and he is not at peace with himself, but he has turned that corner and may do it again.

Peeping Toms and burglars are more furtive than holdup men, as a rule. Robbers are usually broad-faced.

Bigamists often have a rather quiet and velvety and attentive way with women. (The roaming Romeo usually has pride, too, in his personal appearance.)

I asked a high-ranking Los Angeles police officer (a night police chief, now retired) how his personological knowledge had most helped him. He said, "in getting confessions." He knew how to talk in a companionable way to the large-eyed emotional person . . . to explain the reasons *why* to the analytical individual . . . to appeal to the conscience of the narrow-viewed person.

I soon found in my research at San Quentin that there is no criminal type. Every inmate I checked was a very distinct individual. Even the same type of crime would be done very differently by different individuals. But it always added up along the lines of pronounced natural propensities. Very often it was under the influence of dope or alcohol that the person would let go and do what he had only contemplated before.

What is different about criminals is that their traits are

more pronounced, and their control factors less. It is in a prison population that you will most quickly find the most extreme scores on traits. It is a rich, but very disheartening research field. There is a heavy, yet electric atmosphere in and around the Big House. The men are anxious to find out why they let go and did what they did. No man I analyzed denied doing that with which he was charged. With specific personological knowledge, some of them made spectacular success on their paroles. They could divide their traits and conquer the troublesome ones, rather than having to work their whole general being over in some way.

There is not a sharp dichotomy in humanity, with the extremely law-abiding at one end and a group of criminals at the other, and nobody in between. Rather, the build that lets a man go and do what he knows he shouldn't is on a gradient. Traits vary. But control is always possible through free agency. That is a factor that you do not know, even with face language. Control can be built up. That is the divine thing about humans —every one is great at the core. It is just the mechanism of control and expression that has to be directed. Some have more to control than others. Some work harder at it.

Most people you know personally are just great. And the people in the plus-column of contributions to humanity are by far the most numerous. (They have to be, to carry the tax burden of those incarcerated for correction or institutionalized for help.) So while all this is happening, it is good to keep your car and your house locked, go easy on developing contact with persons either shifty-eyed or with a hard, brassy gaze—and associate as much as possible with the heart-of-gold people who are the large majority.

19. IN THE COURTROOM

An El Cerrito, California woman studied a basic structure/ function (personological) course which included facial indicators on traits. Since then she has been helping her husband, an attorney, select jurors—so far, he has had 11 jury cases, and has not lost one.

If you yourself have ever served on a jury in a superior court, and think back on it, it was the jurors with the large eyes and lips and concave noses who wanted to give a large award in an accident case. They were sympathetic. But the hawk-nosed, tight-lipped, small-eyed jurors were less liberal about handing out the insurance company's money.

You may remember, too, that in the judge's instructions to the jury, he mentioned something to the effect that besides considering the words that you heard from witnesses, you should bear in mind the way in which witnesses gave their testimony—whether they appeared to be openly telling the whole truth or not.

What an important example of face language is the courtroom! The experienced and observant attorney has a feel for just the right time to get his point across to the jury and sign off. Also he has observed opposition witnesses and tried to see just how flustered they could become. He has kept alert to the expressions of his own witnesses under cross-examination by opposing counsel, to see how firmly they stood the questioning and whether they needed some help from him in the way of objection to a question.

Facial expressions, tones of voice, flushed or paling skin, a trembling lip, change of breathing pace, frowns, hesitations —all are indicators of the momentary feeling or mood. More basic are the indicators of natural disposition. The broad-faced person is less likely to be shaken. The small-eyed person will remain more matter-of-fact. The tight-lipped person will say volumes in a few words.

The analytical person hates to be forced into a direct "yes" or "no" answer. He would like to explain the whole setup. The hard person is more wooden. The soft, wishy-washy person may get hysterical. The ruggedly-built, heavily textured person can more easily stand being shouted at. The thin-skinned, more baby-haired individual likes gentler treatment. The affable person is more down to earth and at ease. The discriminative, reserved person is more formal. The exacting person, with the worry lines, wants to frame his statement an exact way. And, the dramatic person, especially if broad-faced and in a situation where he feels safe, may put on quite a show. He has a feel for the theatrical.

Attorneys have their traits, too. If the jury needs to be swayed emotionally, you are fortunate if you have a barrister who has just the traits to do it—self-confidence, emotionality, a feel for the dramatic . . . even a touch of humor.

If you happen to be testifying for yourself, you can almost feel the face language of the situation working—the jurors sitting up and paying attention to this new witness, and wondering just what kind of a person you are, as well as listening to what you have to say. You are wise if you appear forthright and direct. Face language is such a constant part of human contact that the jurors are trying to size you up, even if they have never consciously formulated any technique for doing so.

In a high-voltage situation like the courtroom, the unique qualities of individuals stand out in stark relief. The same is true in other intense, vital situations, such as births, deaths and marriages.

Do not wait for such situations to call on your face language knowledge. Utilize it in every situation. *You,* and your pride in yourself are what is important, even if the situation is not.

20. WHAT YOU KNOW AND WHAT YOU DON'T KNOW

Time for inventory!

You now know, or have available to you, 21 valuable concepts of face language . . . complete with indicators . . . for qualities ranging all the way from emotionality to such a fussy trait as exactingness. Also, you know more about temporary expressions of the face—such as not to put too much faith in a person who will not meet your gaze.

All this is a lot to know. Keep it simple. Keep working on outstanding traits—the ones which jump out at you—the ones most distinct about the person. Skip traits which are average. It is the extremes which make the individual. And these extremes are the most easily spotted.

With face language, you have valuable, specific, workable tools—exactly what you read this book to get. You have a place to start with each person.

Of course, there are a lot of things you don't yet know. There are 47 additional personological factors you could learn if you tapped the body of organized knowledge available by

How would you deal with this young fellow in an everyday situation? From your face language, you know he has much courage, warmth, charm, generosity and sincerity—but that also he is critical and not easy to please. Press the right buttons and you will find him a most stimulating companion.

studying in person or by correspondence with the Interstate College of Personology. Face language is a facet of personology, which is the study of how each person is gifted in different ways genetically, and how to best express these traits. The additional traits you could learn range from adventurousness to stubbornness.

There are other factors you don't know about the person. It may very well be you could learn much of interest about his background and experiences . . . his present attitudes and dreams and goals.

But your face language knowledge gives you keys to opening up those broader areas . . . and in a very wholesome, natural way whereby the other individual scarcely gives you a double take, he so much welcomes being approached according to the way *he* is built as an individual.

And—an important spin-off benefit for you: Not only are you more cognizant now of what others' faces tell you . . . you are also more aware of what *your* face tells others! You now know ways to very satisfyingly improve your appearance and image, such as by eliminating worry lines and being sure you have a happy mouth. Either intuitively or consciously, people are busy every day taking you at face value. Whether the value of the dollar skids is out of your personal control, but you can increase deliberately the face value of your own countenance.

A CLOSING WORD

Human beings try to gauge each other by watching the other person's face.

One can gain valuable, specific indications of the other person's nature from this—both from his basic individual structure, and from lines and other indications of patterns of functioning he has built up. Also there are temporary, nonverbal indications of which way he is leaning in the episode of the moment.

In this book you have discovered many of these indications. Freely put to use what you have learned. It will give you more effectiveness in communicating with others, and in persuading them. Also, you will enjoy contact with them more ... you will appreciate them more as individuals—and you will be more tolerant through your greater understanding of them.

Additionally, you have gained some valuable tips about how to best express *yourself* according to your own personal build. The brief rule of thumb is: "Talk to the other person's key trait, and work on your own." Remember, it's always the extreme trait which makes the individual. Skip trait indications which are medium, and direct your attention, your words and actions, to the trait indications that are so obvious that they "jump out at you."

After you have met someone, take a 3 × 5 card and make a list of his key traits. Look at this card, as a refresher, before dealing with him (or her) again.

Let other members of your family read this book, so they will better understand you and harmonize with you (as well as understanding themselves better, and learning to estimate others).

If you notice that some members of your family have traits which make them hard to deal with, or hard for them to accept new information, use your own new knowledge effectively enough and long enough that they notice the favorable difference in you. Then they will be interested in what worked for you.

As pleasant and interesting as this book (and its illustrations) have been for you, the progress you make when applying it will be even more satisfying, in proportion to how much you apply it.

Now move from the vague world of "groups" and enter and enjoy the World of Individuals!